Javascript

The Ultimate Beginner's Guide to Learn Javascript

Disclaimers

We are not lawyers. This website and the content provided herein are simply for educational purposes and do not take the place of legal advice from your attorney. Every effort has been made to ensure that the content provided on this website is accurate and helpful for our readers at publishing time. However, this is not an exhaustive treatment of the subjects. No liability is assumed for losses or damages due to the information provided. You are responsible for your own choices, actions, and results. You should consult your attorney for your specific publishing and disclaimer questions and needs.

Javascript Tutorial

JavaScript is a lightweight, interpreted programming language. It is designed for creating network-centric applications. It is complimentary to and integrated with Java. JavaScript is very easy to implement because it is integrated with HTML. It is open and cross-platform.

Audience

This tutorial has been prepared for JavaScript beginners to help them understand the basic functionality of JavaScript to build dynamic web pages and web applications.

Prerequisites

For this tutorial, it is assumed that the reader have a prior knowledge of HTML coding. It would help if the reader had some prior exposure to object-oriented programming concepts and a general idea on creating online applications.

Table of Contents

JavaScript - Overview

Javascript is a dynamic computer programming language. It is lightweight and most commonly used as a part of web pages, whose implementations allow client-side script to interact with the user and make dynamic pages. It is an interpreted programming language with object-oriented capabilities.

JavaScript was first known as **LiveScript,** but Netscape changed its name to JavaScript, possibly because of the excitement being generated by Java. JavaScript made its first appearance in Netscape 2.0 in 1995 with the name **LiveScript**. The general-purpose core of the language has been embedded in Netscape, Internet Explorer, and other web browsers.

The ECMA-262 Specification defined a standard version of the core JavaScript language.

- JavaScript is a lightweight, interpreted programming language.
- Designed for creating network-centric applications.
- Complementary to and integrated with Java.
- Complementary to and integrated with HTML.
- Open and cross-platform

Client-side JavaScript

Client-side JavaScript is the most common form of the language. The script should be included in or referenced by an HTML document for the code to be interpreted by the browser.

It means that a web page need not be a static HTML, but can include programs that interact with the user, control the browser, and dynamically create HTML content.

The JavaScript client-side mechanism provides many advantages over traditional CGI server-side scripts. For example, you might use JavaScript to check if the user has entered a valid e-mail address in a form field.

The JavaScript code is executed when the user submits the form, and only if all the entries are valid, they would be submitted to the Web Server.

JavaScript can be used to trap user-initiated events such as button clicks, link navigation, and other actions that the user initiates explicitly or implicitly.

Advantages of JavaScript

The merits of using JavaScript are −

- **Less server interaction** − You can validate user input before sending the page off to the server. This saves server traffic, which means less load on your server.

- **Immediate feedback to the visitors** − They don't have to wait for a page reload to see if they have forgotten to enter something.

- **Increased interactivity** − You can create interfaces that react when the user hovers over them with a mouse or activates them via the keyboard.

- **Richer interfaces** − You can use JavaScript to include such items as drag-and-drop components and sliders to give a Rich Interface to your site visitors.

Limitations of JavaScript

We cannot treat JavaScript as a full-fledged programming language. It lacks the following important features –

- Client-side JavaScript does not allow the reading or writing of files. This has been kept for security reason.
- JavaScript cannot be used for networking applications because there is no such support available.
- JavaScript doesn't have any multithreading or multiprocessor capabilities.

Once again, JavaScript is a lightweight, interpreted programming language that allows you to build interactivity into otherwise static HTML pages.

JavaScript Development Tools

One of major strengths of JavaScript is that it does not require expensive development tools. You can start with a simple text editor such as Notepad. Since it is an interpreted language inside the context of a web browser, you don't even need to buy a compiler.

To make our life simpler, various vendors have come up with very nice JavaScript editing tools. Some of them are listed here –

- **Microsoft FrontPage** – Microsoft has developed a popular HTML editor called FrontPage. FrontPage also provides web developers with a number of JavaScript tools to assist in the creation of interactive websites.

- **Macromedia Dreamweaver MX** – Macromedia Dreamweaver MX is a very popular HTML and JavaScript editor in the professional web development crowd. It provides several handy prebuilt JavaScript components, integrates well with databases, and conforms to new standards such as XHTML and XML.

- **Macromedia HomeSite 5** – HomeSite 5 is a well-liked HTML and JavaScript editor from Macromedia that can be used to manage personal websites effectively.

Where is JavaScript Today?

The ECMAScript Edition 5 standard will be the first update to be released in over four years. JavaScript 2.0 conforms to Edition 5 of the ECMAScript standard, and the difference between the two is extremely minor.

The specification for JavaScript 2.0 can be found on the following site: http://www.ecmascript.org/

Today, Netscape's JavaScript and Microsoft's JScript conform to the ECMAScript standard, although both the languages still support the features that are not a part of the standard.

JavaScript - Syntax

JavaScript can be implemented using JavaScript statements that are placed within the **<script>... </script>** HTML tags in a web page.

You can place the **<script>** tags, containing your JavaScript, anywhere within your web page, but it is normally recommended that you should keep it within the **<head>** tags.

The <script> tag alerts the browser program to start interpreting all the text between these tags as a script. A simple syntax of your JavaScript will appear as follows.

```
<script ...>
   JavaScript code
</script>
```

The script tag takes two important attributes −

- **Language** − This attribute specifies what scripting language you are using. Typically, its value will be javascript. Although recent versions of HTML (and XHTML, its successor) have phased out the use of this attribute.

- **Type** − This attribute is what is now recommended to indicate the scripting language in use and its value should be set to "text/javascript".

So your JavaScript segment will look like −

```
<script language="javascript" type="text/javascript">
   JavaScript code
</script>
```

Your First JavaScript Script

Let us take a sample example to print out "Hello World". We added an optional HTML comment that surrounds our JavaScript code. This is to save our code from a browser that does not support JavaScript. The comment ends with a "//-->". Here "//" signifies a comment in JavaScript, so we add that to prevent a browser from reading the end of the HTML comment as a piece of JavaScript code. Next, we call a function **document.write** which writes a string into our HTML document.

This function can be used to write text, HTML, or both. Take a look at the following code.

```html
<html>
    <body>
        <script language="javascript" type="text/javascript">
            <!--
                document.write("Hello World!")
            //-->
        </script>
    </body>
</html>
```

This code will produce the following result −

```
Hello World!
```

Whitespace and Line Breaks

JavaScript ignores spaces, tabs, and newlines that appear in JavaScript programs. You can use spaces, tabs, and newlines freely in your program and you are free to format and indent your programs in a neat and consistent way that makes the code easy to read and understand.

Semicolons are Optional

Simple statements in JavaScript are generally followed by a semicolon character, just as they are in C, C++, and Java. JavaScript, however, allows you to omit this semicolon if each of your statements are placed on a separate line. For example, the following code could be written without semicolons.

```
<script language="javascript" type="text/javascript">
    <!--
        var1 = 10
        var2 = 20
    //-->
</script>
```

But when formatted in a single line as follows, you must use semicolons

-

```
<script language="javascript" type="text/javascript">
    <!--
        var1 = 10; var2 = 20;
    //-->
</script>
```

Note – It is a good programming practice to use semicolons.

Case Sensitivity

JavaScript is a case-sensitive language. This means that the language keywords, variables, function names, and any other identifiers must always be typed with a consistent capitalization of letters.

So the identifiers **Time** and **TIME** will convey different meanings in JavaScript.

NOTE – Care should be taken while writing variable and function names in JavaScript.

Comments in JavaScript

JavaScript supports both C-style and C++-style comments, Thus −

- Any text between a // and the end of a line is treated as a comment and is ignored by JavaScript.
- Any text between the characters /* and */ is treated as a comment. This may span multiple lines.
- JavaScript also recognizes the HTML comment opening sequence <!--. JavaScript treats this as a single-line comment, just as it does the // comment.
- The HTML comment closing sequence --> is not recognized by JavaScript so it should be written as //-->.

Example

The following example shows how to use comments in JavaScript.

```
<script language="javascript" type="text/javascript">
    <!--

    // This is a comment. It is similar to comments in C++

    /*
    * This is a multiline comment in JavaScript
    * It is very similar to comments in C Programming
    */

    //-->
</script>
```

Enabling JavaScript in Browsers

All the modern browsers come with built-in support for JavaScript. Frequently, you may need to enable or disable this support manually. This chapter explains the procedure of enabling and disabling JavaScript support in your browsers: Internet Explorer, Firefox, chrome, and Opera.

JavaScript in Internet Explorer

Here are simple steps to turn on or turn off JavaScript in your Internet Explorer –

- Follow **Tools → Internet Options** from the menu.
- Select **Security** tab from the dialog box.
- Click the **Custom Level** button.
- Scroll down till you find **Scripting option.**
- Select *Enable* radio button under **Active scripting**.
- Finally click OK and come out

To disable JavaScript support in your Internet Explorer, you need to select **Disable** radio button under **Active scripting**.

JavaScript in Firefox

Here are the steps to turn on or turn off JavaScript in Firefox –

- Open a new tab → type **about: config** in the address bar.
- Then you will find the warning dialog. Select **I'll be careful, I promise!**
- Then you will find the list of **configure options** in the browser.
- In the search bar, type **javascript.enabled**.
- There you will find the option to enable or disable javascript by right-clicking on the value of that option → **select toggle**.

If javascript.enabled is true; it converts to false upon clicking **toogle**. If javascript is disabled; it gets enabled upon clicking toggle.

JavaScript in Chrome

Here are the steps to turn on or turn off JavaScript in Chrome –

- Click the Chrome menu at the top right hand corner of your browser.
- Select **Settings**.
- Click **Show advanced settings** at the end of the page.
- Under the **Privacy** section, click the Content settings button.
- In the "Javascript" section, select "Do not allow any site to run JavaScript" or "Allow all sites to run JavaScript (recommended)".

JavaScript in Opera

Here are the steps to turn on or turn off JavaScript in Opera –

- Follow **Tools → Preferences** from the menu.
- Select **Advanced** option from the dialog box.
- Select **Content** from the listed items.
- Select **Enable JavaScript** checkbox.
- Finally click OK and come out.

To disable JavaScript support in your Opera, you should not select the **Enable JavaScript checkbox**.

Warning for Non-JavaScript Browsers

If you have to do something important using JavaScript, then you can display a warning message to the user using **<noscript>** tags.

You can add a **noscript** block immediately after the script block as follows −

```
<html>
   <body>

      <script language="javascript" type="text/javascript">
         <!--
            document.write("Hello World!")
         //-->
      </script>

      <noscript>
         Sorry...JavaScript is needed to go ahead.
      </noscript>

   </body>
</html>
```

Now, if the user's browser does not support JavaScript or JavaScript is not enabled, then the message from </noscript> will be displayed on the screen.

JavaScript - Placement in HTML File

There is a flexibility given to include JavaScript code anywhere in an HTML document. However the most preferred ways to include JavaScript in an HTML file are as follows −

- Script in <head>...</head> section.
- Script in <body>...</body> section.
- Script in <body>...</body> and <head>...</head> sections.
- Script in an external file and then include in <head>...</head> section.

In the following section, we will see how we can place JavaScript in an HTML file in different ways.

JavaScript in \<head\>...\</head\> section

If you want to have a script run on some event, such as when a user clicks somewhere, then you will place that script in the head as follows –

```
<html>

    <head>

        <script type="text/javascript">
            <!--
                function sayHello() {
                    alert("Hello World")
                }
            //-->
        </script>

    </head>

    <body>
        <input type="button" onclick="sayHello()" value="Say
Hello" />
    </body>

</html>
```

This code will produce the following results –

JavaScript in <body>...</body> section

If you need a script to run as the page loads so that the script generates content in the page, then the script goes in the <body> portion of the document. In this case, you would not have any function defined using JavaScript. Take a look at the following code.

```
<html>

    <head>
    </head>

    <body>

        <script type="text/javascript">
            <!--
                document.write("Hello World")
            //-->
        </script>

        <p>This is web page body </p>

    </body>
</html>
```

This code will produce the following results −

JavaScript in \<body\> and \<head\> Sections

You can put your JavaScript code in <head> and <body> section altogether as follows −

```
<html>
   <head>
      <script type="text/javascript">
         <!--
            function sayHello() {
               alert("Hello World")
            }
         //-->
      </script>
   </head>

   <body>
      <script type="text/javascript">
         <!--
            document.write("Hello World")
         //-->
      </script>

      <input type="button" onclick="sayHello()" value="Say
Hello" />

   </body>
</html>
```

This code will produce the following result −

JavaScript in External File

As you begin to work more extensively with JavaScript, you will be likely to find that there are cases where you are reusing identical JavaScript code on multiple pages of a site.

You are not restricted to be maintaining identical code in multiple HTML files. The **script** tag provides a mechanism to allow you to store JavaScript in an external file and then include it into your HTML files.

Here is an example to show how you can include an external JavaScript file in your HTML code using **script** tag and its **src** attribute.

```
<html>

    <head>
        <script type="text/javascript" src="filename.js"
></script>
    </head>

    <body>
        .......
    </body>
</html>
```

To use JavaScript from an external file source, you need to write all your JavaScript source code in a simple text file with the extension ".js" and then include that file as shown above.

For example, you can keep the following content in **filename.js** file and then you can use **sayHello** function in your HTML file after including the filename.js file.

```
function sayHello() {
    alert("Hello World")
}
```

JavaScript – Variables

JavaScript Datatypes

One of the most fundamental characteristics of a programming language is the set of data types it supports. These are the type of values that can be represented and manipulated in a programming language.

JavaScript allows you to work with three primitive data types –

- **Numbers,** eg. 123, 120.50 etc.
- **Strings** of text e.g. "This text string" etc.
- **Boolean** e.g. true or false.

JavaScript also defines two trivial data types, **null** and **undefined,** each of which defines only a single value. In addition to these primitive data types, JavaScript supports a composite data type known as **object**. We will cover objects in detail in a separate chapter.

Note – Java does not make a distinction between integer values and floating-point values. All numbers in JavaScript are represented as floating-point values. JavaScript represents numbers using the 64-bit floating-point format defined by the IEEE 754 standard.

JavaScript Variables

Like many other programming languages, JavaScript has variables. Variables can be thought of as named containers. You can place data into these containers and then refer to the data simply by naming the container.

Before you use a variable in a JavaScript program, you must declare it. Variables are declared with the **var** keyword as follows.

```
<script type="text/javascript">
  <!--
    var money;
    var name;
  //-->
</script>
```

You can also declare multiple variables with the same **var** keyword as follows −

```
<script type="text/javascript">
  <!--
    var money, name;
  //-->
</script>
```

Storing a value in a variable is called **variable initialization**. You can do variable initialization at the time of variable creation or at a later point in time when you need that variable.

For instance, you might create a variable named **money** and assign the value 2000.50 to it later. For another variable, you can assign a value at the time of initialization as follows.

```
<script type="text/javascript">
  <!--
     var name = "Ali";
     var money;
     money = 2000.50;
  //-->
</script>
```

Note – Use the **var** keyword only for declaration or initialization, once for the life of any variable name in a document. You should not re-declare same variable twice.

JavaScript is **untyped** language. This means that a JavaScript variable can hold a value of any data type. Unlike many other languages, you don't have to tell JavaScript during variable declaration what type of value the variable will hold. The value type of a variable can change during the execution of a program and JavaScript takes care of it automatically.

JavaScript Variable Scope

The scope of a variable is the region of your program in which it is defined. JavaScript variables have only two scopes.

- **Global Variables** – A global variable has global scope which means it can be defined anywhere in your JavaScript code.

- **Local Variables** – A local variable will be visible only within a function where it is defined. Function parameters are always local to that function.

Within the body of a function, a local variable takes precedence over a global variable with the same name. If you declare a local variable or function parameter with the same name as a global variable, you effectively hide the global variable. Take a look into the following example.

```
<script type="text/javascript">
    <!--
        var myVar = "global"; // Declare a global variable
        function checkscope( ) {
            var myVar = "local";   // Declare a local variable
            document.write(myVar);
        }
    //-->
</script>
```

This produces the following result –

```
local
```

JavaScript Variable Names

While naming your variables in JavaScript, keep the following rules in mind.

- You should not use any of the JavaScript reserved keywords as a variable name. These keywords are mentioned in the next section. For example, **break** or **boolean** variable names are not valid.
- JavaScript variable names should not start with a numeral (0-9). They must begin with a letter or an underscore character. For example, **123test** is an invalid variable name but **_123test** is a valid one.
- JavaScript variable names are case-sensitive. For example, **Name** and **name** are two different variables.

JavaScript Reserved Words

A list of all the reserved words in JavaScript are given in the following table. They cannot be used as JavaScript variables, functions, methods, loop labels, or any object names.

abstract	else	instanceof	switch
boolean	enum	int	synchronized
break	export	interface	this
byte	extends	long	throw
case	false	native	throws
catch	final	new	transient
char	finally	null	true
class	float	package	try
const	for	private	typeof
continue	function	protected	var
debugger	goto	public	void
default	if	return	volatile
delete	implements	short	while
do	import	static	with
double	in	super	

JavaScript - Operators

What is an operator?

Let us take a simple expression **4 + 5 is equal to 9**. Here 4 and 5 are called **operands** and '+' is called the **operator**. JavaScript supports the following types of operators.

- Arithmetic Operators
- Comparision Operators
- Logical (or Relational) Operators
- Assignment Operators
- Conditional (or ternary) Operators

Lets have a look on all operators one by one.

Arithmetic Operators

JavaScript supports the following arithmetic operators −

Assume variable A holds 10 and variable B holds 20, then −

Sr.No	Operator and Description
1	**+ (Addition)** Adds two operands **Ex:** A + B will give 30

2	**- (Subtraction)** Subtracts the second operand from the first **Ex:** A - B will give -10
3	*** (Multiplication)** Multiply both operands **Ex:** A * B will give 200
4	**/ (Division)** Divide the numerator by the denominator **Ex:** B / A will give 2
5	**% (Modulus)** Outputs the remainder of an integer division **Ex:** B % A will give 0
6	**++ (Increment)** Increases an integer value by one **Ex:** A++ will give 11
7	**-- (Decrement)** Decreases an integer value by one **Ex:** A-- will give 9

Note – Addition operator (+) works for Numeric as well as Strings. e.g. "a" + 10 will give "a10".

Example

The following code shows how to use arithmetic operators in JavaScript.

```html
<html>
   <body>

      <script type="text/javascript">
         <!--
            var a = 33;
            var b = 10;
            var c = "Test";
            var linebreak = "<br />";

            document.write("a + b = ");
            result = a + b;
            document.write(result);
            document.write(linebreak);

            document.write("a - b = ");
            result = a - b;
            document.write(result);
            document.write(linebreak);

            document.write("a / b = ");
            result = a / b;
            document.write(result);
            document.write(linebreak);

            document.write("a % b = ");
            result = a % b;
            document.write(result);
            document.write(linebreak);
```

```
        document.write("a + b + c = ");
        result = a + b + c;
        document.write(result);
        document.write(linebreak);

        a = a++;
        document.write("a++ = ");
        result = a++;
        document.write(result);
        document.write(linebreak);

        b = b--;
        document.write("b-- = ");
        result = b--;
        document.write(result);
        document.write(linebreak);
    //-->
    </script>

    Set the variables to different values and then try...
  </body>
</html>
```

Output

```
a + b = 43
a - b = 23
a / b = 3.3
a % b = 3
a + b + c = 43Test
a++ = 33
b-- = 10
Set the variables to different values and then try...
```

Comparison Operators

JavaScript supports the following comparison operators –

Assume variable A holds 10 and variable B holds 20, then –

Sr.No	Operator and Description
1	**= = (Equal)** Checks if the value of two operands are equal or not, if yes, then the condition becomes true. **Ex:** (A == B) is not true.
2	**!= (Not Equal)** Checks if the value of two operands are equal or not, if the values are not equal, then the condition becomes true. **Ex:** (A != B) is true.
3	**> (Greater than)** Checks if the value of the left operand is greater than the value of the right operand, if yes, then the condition becomes true. **Ex:** (A > B) is not true.

4	**< (Less than)**
	Checks if the value of the left operand is less than the value of the right operand, if yes, then the condition becomes true.
	Ex: (A < B) is true.

5	**>= (Greater than or Equal to)**
	Checks if the value of the left operand is greater than or equal to the value of the right operand, if yes, then the condition becomes true.
	Ex: (A >= B) is not true.

6	**<= (Less than or Equal to)**
	Checks if the value of the left operand is less than or equal to the value of the right operand, if yes, then the condition becomes true.
	Ex: (A <= B) is true.

Example

The following code shows how to use comparison operators in JavaScript.

```html
<html>
  <body>

    <script type="text/javascript">
      <!--
        var a = 10;
        var b = 20;
        var linebreak = "<br />";

        document.write("(a == b) => ");
        result = (a == b);
        document.write(result);
        document.write(linebreak);

        document.write("(a < b) => ");
        result = (a < b);
        document.write(result);
        document.write(linebreak);

        document.write("(a > b) => ");
        result = (a > b);
        document.write(result);
        document.write(linebreak);

        document.write("(a != b) => ");
        result = (a != b);
        document.write(result);
        document.write(linebreak);

        document.write("(a >= b) => ");
        result = (a >= b);
        document.write(result);
```

```
        document.write(linebreak);

        document.write("(a <= b) => ");
        result = (a <= b);
        document.write(result);
        document.write(linebreak);
    //-->
    </script>
```

    Set the variables to different values and different
operators and then try...
    </body>
</html>

Output

```
(a == b) => false
(a < b) => true
(a > b) => false
(a != b) => true
(a >= b) => false
a <= b) => true
```
Set the variables to different values and different operators and then
try...

Logical Operators

JavaScript supports the following logical operators −

Assume variable A holds 10 and variable B holds 20, then −

Sr.No	Operator and Description
1	**&& (Logical AND)** If both the operands are non-zero, then the condition becomes true. **Ex:** (A && B) is true.
2	**|| (Logical OR)** If any of the two operands are non-zero, then the condition becomes true. **Ex:** (A || B) is true.
3	**! (Logical NOT)** Reverses the logical state of its operand. If a condition is true, then the Logical NOT operator will make it false. **Ex:** ! (A && B) is false.

Example

Try the following code to learn how to implement Logical Operators in JavaScript.

```html
<html>
   <body>

      <script type="text/javascript">
         <!--
            var a = true;
            var b = false;
            var linebreak = "<br />";

            document.write("(a && b) => ");
            result = (a && b);
            document.write(result);
            document.write(linebreak);

            document.write("(a || b) => ");
            result = (a || b);
            document.write(result);
            document.write(linebreak);

            document.write("!(a && b) => ");
            result = (!(a && b));
            document.write(result);
            document.write(linebreak);
         //-->
      </script>

      <p>Set the variables to different values and different operators and then try...</p>
   </body>
</html>
```

Output

```
(a && b) => false
(a || b) => true
!(a && b) => true
Set the variables to different values and different operators and then
try...
```

Bitwise Operators

JavaScript supports the following bitwise operators −

Assume variable A holds 2 and variable B holds 3, then −

Sr.No	Operator and Description
1	**& (Bitwise AND)** It performs a Boolean AND operation on each bit of its integer arguments. **Ex:** (A & B) is 2.
2	**| (BitWise OR)** It performs a Boolean OR operation on each bit of its integer arguments. **Ex:** (A | B) is 3.
3	**^ (Bitwise XOR)** It performs a Boolean exclusive OR operation on each bit of its integer arguments. Exclusive OR means that either operand one is true or operand two is true, but not both. **Ex:** (A ^ B) is 1.

4	**~ (Bitwise Not)** It is a unary operator and operates by reversing all the bits in the operand. **Ex:** (~B) is -4.
5	**<< (Left Shift)** It moves all the bits in its first operand to the left by the number of places specified in the second operand. New bits are filled with zeros. Shifting a value left by one position is equivalent to multiplying it by 2, shifting two positions is equivalent to multiplying by 4, and so on. **Ex:** (A << 1) is 4.
6	**>> (Right Shift)** Binary Right Shift Operator. The left operand's value is moved right by the number of bits specified by the right operand. **Ex:** (A >> 1) is 1.
7	**>>> (Right shift with Zero)** This operator is just like the >> operator, except that the bits shifted in on the left are always zero. **Ex:** (A >>> 1) is 1.

Example

Try the following code to implement Bitwise operator in JavaScript.

```
<html>
    <body>

        <script type="text/javascript">
        <!--
            var a = 2; // Bit presentation 10
            var b = 3; // Bit presentation 11
            var linebreak = "<br />";

            document.write("(a & b) => ");
            result = (a & b);
            document.write(result);
            document.write(linebreak);

            document.write("(a | b) => ");
            result = (a | b);
            document.write(result);
            document.write(linebreak);

            document.write("(a ^ b) => ");
            result = (a ^ b);
            document.write(result);
            document.write(linebreak);

            document.write("(~b) => ");
            result = (~b);
            document.write(result);
            document.write(linebreak);

            document.write("(a << b) => ");
            result = (a << b);
            document.write(result);
```

```
        document.write(linebreak);

        document.write("(a >> b) => ");
        result = (a >> b);
        document.write(result);
        document.write(linebreak);
      //-->
    </script>

      <p>Set the variables to different values and different
operators and then try...</p>
    </body>
</html>
```

```
(a & b) => 2
(a | b) => 3
(a ^ b) => 1
(~b) => -4
(a << b) => 16
(a >> b) => 0
Set the variables to different values and different operators and then
try...
```

Assignment Operators

JavaScript supports the following assignment operators –

Sr.No	Operator and Description
1	**= (Simple Assignment)** Assigns values from the right side operand to the left side operand **Ex:** C = A + B will assign the value of A + B into C
2	**+= (Add and Assignment)** It adds the right operand to the left operand and assigns the result to the left operand. **Ex:** C += A is equivalent to C = C + A
3	**-= (Subtract and Assignment)** It subtracts the right operand from the left operand and assigns the result to the left operand. **Ex:** C -= A is equivalent to C = C - A

4	***= (Multiply and Assignment)** It multiplies the right operand with the left operand and assigns the result to the left operand. **Ex:** C *= A is equivalent to C = C * A
5	**/= (Divide and Assignment)** It divides the left operand with the right operand and assigns the result to the left operand. **Ex:** C /= A is equivalent to C = C / A
6	**%= (Modules and Assignment)** It takes modulus using two operands and assigns the result to the left operand. **Ex:** C %= A is equivalent to C = C % A

Note – Same logic applies to Bitwise operators so they will become like

<<=, >>=, >>=, &=, |= and ^=.

Example

Try the following code to implement assignment operator in JavaScript.

```html
<html>
  <body>

    <script type="text/javascript">
      <!--
        var a = 33;
        var b = 10;
        var linebreak = "<br />";

        document.write("Value of a => (a = b) => ");
        result = (a = b);
        document.write(result);
        document.write(linebreak);

        document.write("Value of a => (a += b) => ");
        result = (a += b);
        document.write(result);
        document.write(linebreak);

        document.write("Value of a => (a -= b) => ");
        result = (a -= b);
        document.write(result);
        document.write(linebreak);

        document.write("Value of a => (a *= b) => ");
        result = (a *= b);
        document.write(result);
        document.write(linebreak);

        document.write("Value of a => (a /= b) => ");
        result = (a /= b);
        document.write(result);
```

```
        document.write(linebreak);

        document.write("Value of a => (a %= b) => ");
        result = (a %= b);
        document.write(result);
        document.write(linebreak);
    //-->
    </script>

        <p>Set the variables to different values and different
operators and then try...</p>
    </body>
</html>
```

Output

Value of a => (a = b) => 10
Value of a => (a += b) => 20
Value of a => (a -= b) => 10
Value of a => (a *= b) => 100
Value of a => (a /= b) => 10
Value of a => (a %= b) => 0
Set the variables to different values and different operators and then
try...

Miscellaneous Operator

We will discuss two operators here that are quite useful in JavaScript: the **conditional operator** (? :) and the **typeof operator**.

Conditional Operator (? :)

The conditional operator first evaluates an expression for a true or false value and then executes one of the two given statements depending upon the result of the evaluation.

Sr.No	Operator and Description
1	**? : (Conditional)** If Condition is true? Then value X : Otherwise value Y

Example

Try the following code to understand how the Conditional Operator works in JavaScript.

```html
<html>
   <body>

      <script type="text/javascript">
         <!--
            var a = 10;
            var b = 20;
            var linebreak = "<br />";

            document.write ("((a > b) ? 100 : 200) => ");
            result = (a > b) ? 100 : 200;
            document.write(result);
            document.write(linebreak);

            document.write ("((a < b) ? 100 : 200) => ");
            result = (a < b) ? 100 : 200;
            document.write(result);
            document.write(linebreak);
         //-->
      </script>

      <p>Set the variables to different values and different
operators and then try...</p>
   </body>
</html>
```

Output

```
((a > b) ? 100 : 200) => 200
((a < b) ? 100 : 200) => 100
Set the variables to different values and different operators and then
try...
```

typeof Operator

The **typeof** operator is a unary operator that is placed before its single operand, which can be of any type. Its value is a string indicating the data type of the operand.

The *typeof* operator evaluates to "number", "string", or "boolean" if its operand is a number, string, or boolean value and returns true or false based on the evaluation.Here is a list of the return values for the **typeof** Operator.

Type	String Returned by typeof
Number	"number"
String	"string"
Boolean	"boolean"
Object	"object"
Function	"function"
Undefined	"undefined"
Null	"object"

Example

The following code shows how to implement **typeof** operator.

```html
<html>
   <body>

      <script type="text/javascript">
         <!--
            var a = 10;
            var b = "String";
            var linebreak = "<br />";
            result = (typeof b == "string" ? "B is String" : "B
is Numeric");
            document.write("Result => ");
            document.write(result);
            document.write(linebreak);

            result = (typeof a == "string" ? "A is String" : "A
is Numeric");
            document.write("Result => ");
            document.write(result);
            document.write(linebreak);
         //-->
      </script>

      <p>Set the variables to different values and different
operators and then try...</p>
   </body>
</html>
```

Output

```
Result => B is String
Result => A is Numeric
Set the variables to different values and different operators and then
try...
```

JavaScript - if...else Statement

While writing a program, there may be a situation when you need to adopt one out of a given set of paths. In such cases, you need to use conditional statements that allow your program to make correct decisions and perform right actions.

JavaScript supports conditional statements which are used to perform different actions based on different conditions. Here we will explain the **if..else** statement.

Flow Chart of if-else

The following flow chart shows how the if-else statement works.

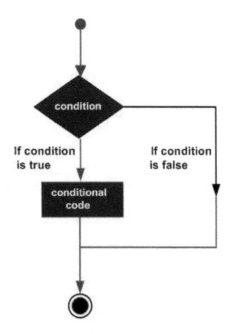

JavaScript supports the following forms of **if..else** statement −

- if statement
- if...else statement
- if...else if... statement.

if statement

The **if** statement is the fundamental control statement that allows JavaScript to make decisions and execute statements conditionally.

Syntax

The syntax for a basic if statement is as follows −

```
if (expression){
    Statement(s) to be executed if expression is true
}
```

Here a JavaScript expression is evaluated. If the resulting value is true, the given statement(s) are executed. If the expression is false, then no statement would be not executed. Most of the times, you will use comparison operators while making decisions.

Example

Try the following example to understand how the **if** statement works.

```html
<html>
  <body>

      <script type="text/javascript">
        <!--
           var age = 20;

           if( age > 18 ){
              document.write("<b>Qualifies for driving</b>");
           }
        //-->
      </script>

      <p>Set the variable to different value and then
try...</p>
  </body>
</html>
```

Output

```
Qualifies for driving
Set the variable to different value and then try...
```

if...else statement:

The **'if...else'** statement is the next form of control statement that allows JavaScript to execute statements in a more controlled way.

Syntax

```
if (expression){
    Statement(s) to be executed if expression is true
}

else{
    Statement(s) to be executed if expression is false
}
```

Here JavaScript expression is evaluated. If the resulting value is true, the given statement(s) in the 'if' block, are executed. If the expression is false, then the given statement(s) in the else block are executed.

Example

Try the following code to learn how to implement an if-else statement in JavaScript.

```html
<html>
   <body>

      <script type="text/javascript">
         <!--
            var age = 15;

            if( age > 18 ){
               document.write("<b>Qualifies for driving</b>");
            }

            else{
               document.write("<b>Does not qualify for
driving</b>");
            }
         //-->
      </script>

      <p>Set the variable to different value and then
try...</p>
   </body>
</html>
```

Output

```
Does not qualify for driving
Set the variable to different value and then try...
```

if...else if... statement

The **if...else if...** statement is an advanced form of **if...else** that allows JavaScript to make a correct decision out of several conditions.

Syntax

The syntax of an if-else-if statement is as follows –

```
if (expression 1){
    Statement(s) to be executed if expression 1 is true
}
else if (expression 2){
    Statement(s) to be executed if expression 2 is true
}
else if (expression 3){
    Statement(s) to be executed if expression 3 is true
}
else{
    Statement(s) to be executed if no expression is true
}
```

There is nothing special about this code. It is just a series of **if** statements, where each **if** is a part of the **else** clause of the previous statement. Statement(s) are executed based on the true condition, if none of the conditions is true, then the **else** block is executed.

Example

Try the following code to learn how to implement an if-else-if statement in JavaScript.

```html
<html>
    <body>

        <script type="text/javascript">
            <!--
                var book = "maths";
                if( book == "history" ){
                    document.write("<b>History Book</b>");
                }
                else if( book == "maths" ){
                    document.write("<b>Maths Book</b>");
                }
                else if( book == "economics" ){
                    document.write("<b>Economics Book</b>");
                }
                else{
                    document.write("<b>Unknown Book</b>");
                }
            //-->
        </script>

        <p>Set the variable to different value and then
try...</p>
    </body>
<html>
```

Output

Maths Book
Set the variable to different value and then try...

JavaScript - Switch Case

You can use multiple **if...else...if** statements, as in the previous chapter, to perform a multiway branch. However, this is not always the best solution, especially when all of the branches depend on the value of a single variable.

Starting with JavaScript 1.2, you can use a **switch** statement which handles exactly this situation, and it does so more efficiently than repeated **if...else if**statements.

Flow Chart

The following flow chart explains a switch-case statement works.

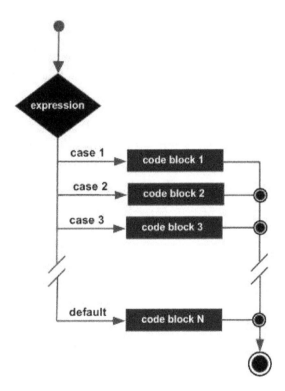

Syntax

The objective of a **switch** statement is to give an expression to evaluate and several different statements to execute based on the value of the expression. The interpreter checks each **case** against the value of the expression until a match is found. If nothing matches, a **default** condition will be used.

```
switch (expression)
{
    case condition 1: statement(s)
    break;

    case condition 2: statement(s)
    break;
    ...

    case condition n: statement(s)
    break;

    default: statement(s)
}
```

The **break** statements indicate the end of a particular case. If they were omitted, the interpreter would continue executing each statement in each of the following cases.

We will explain **break** statement in *Loop Control* chapter.

Example

Try the following example to implement switch-case statement.

```html
<html>
   <body>

      <script type="text/javascript">
         <!--
            var grade='A';
            document.write("Entering switch block<br />");
            switch (grade)
            {
               case 'A': document.write("Good job<br />");
               break;

               case 'B': document.write("Pretty good<br />");
               break;

               case 'C': document.write("Passed<br />");
               break;

               case 'D': document.write("Not so good<br />");
               break;

               case 'F': document.write("Failed<br />");
               break;

               default:  document.write("Unknown grade<br />")
            }
            document.write("Exiting switch block");
         //-->
      </script>

      <p>Set the variable to different value and then
try...</p>
```

```
    </body>
</html>
```

Output

```
Entering switch block
Good job
Exiting switch block
Set the variable to different value and then try...
```

Break statements play a major role in switch-case statements.
Try the following code that uses switch-case statement without
any break statement.

```html
<html>
    <body>

        <script type="text/javascript">
            <!--
                var grade='A';
                document.write("Entering switch block<br />");
                switch (grade)
                {
                    case 'A': document.write("Good job<br />");
                    case 'B': document.write("Pretty good<br />");
                    case 'C': document.write("Passed<br />");
                    case 'D': document.write("Not so good<br />");
                    case 'F': document.write("Failed<br />");
                    default: document.write("Unknown grade<br />")
                }
                document.write("Exiting switch block");
            //-->
        </script>

        <p>Set the variable to different value and then
try...</p>
```

```
    </body>
</html>
```

Output

```
Entering switch block
Good job
Pretty good
Passed
Not so good
Failed
Unknown grade
Exiting switch block
Set the variable to different value and then try...
```

JavaScript - While Loops

While writing a program, you may encounter a situation where you need to perform an action over and over again. In such situations, you would need to write loop statements to reduce the number of lines.

JavaScript supports all the necessary loops to ease down the pressure of programming.

The while Loop

The most basic loop in JavaScript is the **while** loop which would be discussed in this chapter. The purpose of a **while** loop is to execute a statement or code block repeatedly as long as an **expression** is true. Once the expression becomes **false,** the loop terminates.

Flow Chart

The flow chart of **while loop** looks as follows –

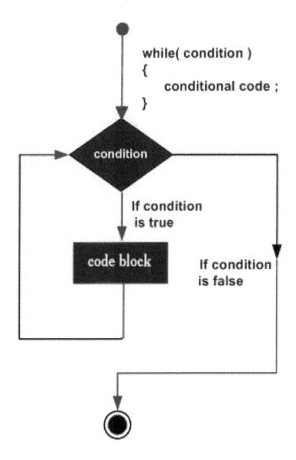

Syntax

The syntax of **while loop** in JavaScript is as follows –

```
while (expression){
    Statement(s) to be executed if expression is true
}
```

Example

Try the following example to implement while loop.

```html
<html>
    <body>

        <script type="text/javascript">
            <!--
                var count = 0;
                document.write("Starting Loop ");

                while (count < 10){
                    document.write("Current Count : " + count + "<br
/>");
                    count++;
                }

                document.write("Loop stopped!");
            //-->
        </script>

        <p>Set the variable to different value and then
try...</p>
    </body>
</html>
```

Output

```
Starting Loop
Current Count : 0
Current Count : 1
Current Count : 2
Current Count : 3
Current Count : 4
Current Count : 5
Current Count : 6
Current Count : 7
Current Count : 8
Current Count : 9
Loop stopped!
Set the variable to different value and then try...
```

The do...while Loop

The **do...while** loop is similar to the **while** loop except that the condition check happens at the end of the loop. This means that the loop will always be executed at least once, even if the condition is **false**.

Flow Chart

The flow chart of a **do-while** loop would be as follows –

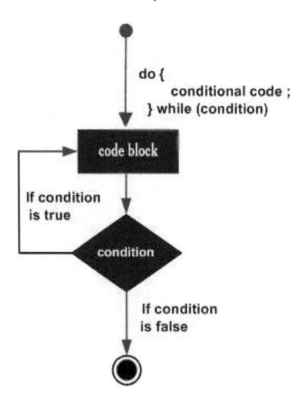

Syntax

The syntax for **do-while** loop in JavaScript is as follows −

```
do{
    Statement(s) to be executed;
} while (expression);
```

Note − Don't miss the semicolon used at the end of the do...while loop.

Example

Try the following example to learn how to implement a **do-while** loop in JavaScript.

```
<html>
    <body>
        <script type="text/javascript">
            <!--
                var count = 0;

                document.write("Starting Loop" + "<br />");
                do{
                    document.write("Current Count : " + count + "<br
/>");
                    count++;
                }
                while (count < 5);
                document.write ("Loop stopped!");
            //-->
        </script>

        <p>Set the variable to different value and then
try...</p>
    </body>
</html>
```

Output

```
Starting Loop
Current Count : 0
Current Count : 1
Current Count : 2
Current Count : 3
Current Count : 4
Loop Stopped!
Set the variable to different value and then try...
```

JavaScript - For Loop

The **'for'** loop is the most compact form of looping. It includes the following three important parts −

- The **loop initialization** where we initialize our counter to a starting value. The initialization statement is executed before the loop begins.
- The **test statement** which will test if a given condition is true or not. If the condition is true, then the code given inside the loop will be executed, otherwise the control will come out of the loop.
- The **iteration statement** where you can increase or decrease your counter.

You can put all the three parts in a single line separated by semicolons.

Flow Chart

The flow chart of a for loop in JavaScript would be as follows –

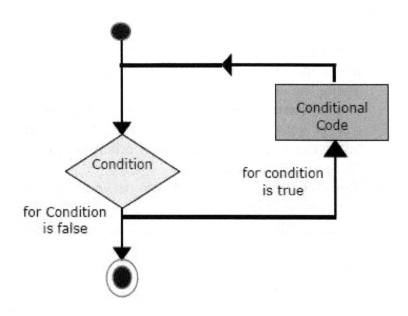

Syntax

The syntax of for loop is JavaScript is as follows –

```
for (initialization; test condition; iteration statement){
   Statement(s) to be executed if test condition is true
}
```

Example

Try the following example to learn how a for loop works in JavaScript.

```html
<html>
   <body>

      <script type="text/javascript">
         <!--
            var count;
            document.write("Starting Loop" + "<br />");

            for(count = 0; count < 10; count++){
               document.write("Current Count : " + count );
               document.write("<br />");
            }

            document.write("Loop stopped!");
         //-->
      </script>

      <p>Set the variable to different value and then
try...</p>
   </body>
</html>
```

Output

```
Starting Loop
Current Count : 0
Current Count : 1
Current Count : 2
Current Count : 3
Current Count : 4
Current Count : 5
Current Count : 6
Current Count : 7
Current Count : 8
Current Count : 9
Loop stopped!
Set the variable to different value and then try...
```

JavaScript for...in loop

The **for...in** loop is used to loop through an object's properties. As we have not discussed Objects yet, you may not feel comfortable with this loop. But once you understand how objects behave in JavaScript, you will find this loop very useful.

Syntax

```
for (variablename in object){
    statement or block to execute
}
```

In each iteration, one property from **object** is assigned to **variablename** and this loop continues till all the properties of the object are exhausted.

Example

Try the following example to implement 'for-in' loop. It prints the web browser's **Navigator** object.

```
<html>
    <body>

        <script type="text/javascript">
            <!--
                var aProperty;
                document.write("Navigator Object Properties<br />
");

                for (aProperty in navigator) {
                    document.write(aProperty);
                    document.write("<br />");
                }
                document.write ("Exiting from the loop!");
```

75

```
    //-->
   </script>

   <p>Set the variable to different object and then
try...</p>
   </body>
</html>
```

Output

```
Navigator Object Properties
serviceWorker
webkitPersistentStorage
webkitTemporaryStorage
geolocation
doNotTrack
onLine
languages
language
userAgent
product
platform
appVersion
appName
appCodeName
hardwareConcurrency
maxTouchPoints
vendorSub
vendor
productSub
cookieEnabled
mimeTypes
plugins
javaEnabled
getStorageUpdates
getGamepads
webkitGetUserMedia
vibrate
getBattery
sendBeacon
```

```
registerProtocolHandler
unregisterProtocolHandler
Exiting from the loop!
Set the variable to different object and then try...
```

JavaScript - Loop Control

JavaScript provides full control to handle loops and switch statements. There may be a situation when you need to come out of a loop without reaching its bottom. There may also be a situation when you want to skip a part of your code block and start the next iteration of the loop.

To handle all such situations, JavaScript provides **break** and **continue**statements. These statements are used to immediately come out of any loop or to start the next iteration of any loop respectively.

The break Statement

The **break** statement, which was briefly introduced with the *switch* statement, is used to exit a loop early, breaking out of the enclosing curly braces.

Flow Chart

The flow chart of a break statement would look as follows –

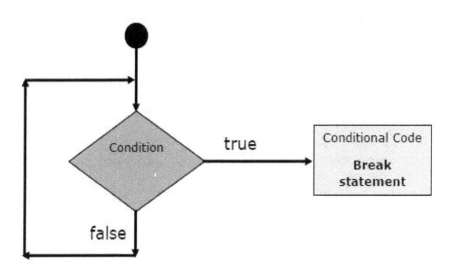

Example

The following example illustrates the use of a **break** statement with a while loop. Notice how the loop breaks out early once **x** reaches 5 and reaches to **document.write (..)** statement just below to the closing curly brace –

```
<html>
    <body>

        <script type="text/javascript">
        <!--
        var x = 1;
        document.write("Entering the loop<br /> ");
```

```
        while (x < 20)
        {
            if (x == 5){
                break; // breaks out of loop completely
            }
            x = x + 1;
            document.write( x + "<br />");
        }

        document.write("Exiting the loop!<br /> ");
        //-->
    </script>

    <p>Set the variable to different value and then
try...</p>
    </body>
</html>
```

Output

```
Entering the loop
2
3
4
5
Exiting the loop!
Set the variable to different value and then try...
```

We already have seen the usage of **break** statement inside **a
switch**statement.

The continue Statement

The **continue** statement tells the interpreter to immediately start the next iteration of the loop and skip the remaining code block. When a **continue**statement is encountered, the program flow moves to the loop check expression immediately and if the condition remains true, then it starts the next iteration, otherwise the control comes out of the loop.

Example

This example illustrates the use of a **continue** statement with a while loop. Notice how the **continue** statement is used to skip printing when the index held in variable **x** reaches 5 –

```html
<html>
   <body>

      <script type="text/javascript">
         <!--
            var x = 1;
            document.write("Entering the loop<br /> ");

            while (x < 10)
            {
               x = x + 1;

               if (x == 5){
                  continue; // skip rest of the loop body
               }
               document.write( x + "<br />");
            }

            document.write("Exiting the loop!<br /> ");
         //-->
```

```
    </script>

        <p>Set the variable to different value and then
try...</p>
    </body>
</html>
```

Output

```
Entering the loop
2
3
4
6
7
8
9
10
Exiting the loop!
```

Using Labels to Control the Flow

Starting from JavaScript 1.2, a label can be used with **break** and **continue** to control the flow more precisely. A **label** is simply an identifier followed by a colon (:) that is applied to a statement or a block of code. We will see two different examples to understand how to use labels with break and continue.

Note – Line breaks are not allowed between the **'continue'** or **'break'**statement and its label name. Also, there should not be any other statement in between a label name and associated loop.

Try the following two examples for a better understanding of Labels.

Example 1

The following example shows how to implement Label with a break statement.

```
<html>
    <body>

        <script type="text/javascript">
            <!--
                document.write("Entering the loop!<br /> ");
                outerloop: // This is the label name

                for (var i = 0; i < 5; i++)
                {
                    document.write("Outerloop: " + i + "<br />");
                    innerloop:
                    for (var j = 0; j < 5; j++)
```

```
                {
                    if (j > 3 ) break ; // Quit the innermost
loop
                    if (i == 2) break innerloop; // Do the same
thing
                    if (i == 4) break outerloop; // Quit the
outer loop
                    document.write("Innerloop: " + j + " <br
/>");
                }
            }

            document.write("Exiting the loop!<br /> ");
        //-->
        </script>

    </body>
</html>
```

Output

```
Entering the loop!
Outerloop: 0
Innerloop: 0
Innerloop: 1
Innerloop: 2
Innerloop: 3
Outerloop: 1
Innerloop: 0
Innerloop: 1
Innerloop: 2
Innerloop: 3
Outerloop: 2
Outerloop: 3
Innerloop: 0
Innerloop: 1
Innerloop: 2
Innerloop: 3
Outerloop: 4
```

Exiting the loop!

Example 2

```
<html>
  <body>

    <script type="text/javascript">
    <!--
    document.write("Entering the loop!<br /> ");
    outerloop: // This is the label name

    for (var i = 0; i < 3; i++)
    {
        document.write("Outerloop: " + i + "<br />");
        for (var j = 0; j < 5; j++)
        {
            if (j == 3){
                continue outerloop;
            }
            document.write("Innerloop: " + j + "<br />");
        }
    }

    document.write("Exiting the loop!<br /> ");
    //-->
    </script>

  </body>
</html>
```

Output

```
Entering the loop!
Outerloop: 0
Innerloop: 0
Innerloop: 1
Innerloop: 2
Outerloop: 1
Innerloop: 0
Innerloop: 1
Innerloop: 2
Outerloop: 2
Innerloop: 0
Innerloop: 1
Innerloop: 2
Exiting the loop!
```

JavaScript - Functions

A function is a group of reusable code which can be called anywhere in your program. This eliminates the need of writing the same code again and again. It helps programmers in writing modular codes. Functions allow a programmer to divide a big program into a number of small and manageable functions.

Like any other advanced programming language, JavaScript also supports all the features necessary to write modular code using functions. You must have seen functions like **alert()** and **write()** in the earlier chapters. We were using these functions again and again, but they had been written in core JavaScript only once.

JavaScript allows us to write our own functions as well. This section explains how to write your own functions in JavaScript.

Function Definition

Before we use a function, we need to define it. The most common way to define a function in JavaScript is by using the **function** keyword, followed by a unique function name, a list of parameters (that might be empty), and a statement block surrounded by curly braces.

Syntax

The basic syntax is shown here.

```
<script type="text/javascript">
    <!--
        function functionname(parameter-list)
        {
            statements
        }
    //-->
</script>
```

Example

Try the following example. It defines a function called sayHello that takes no parameters –

```
<script type="text/javascript">
    <!--
        function sayHello()
        {
            alert("Hello there");
        }
    //-->
</script>
```

Calling a Function

To invoke a function somewhere later in the script, you would simply need to write the name of that function as shown in the following code.

```html
<html>
    <head>

        <script type="text/javascript">
            function sayHello()
            {
                document.write ("Hello there!");
            }
        </script>

    </head>
    <body>
        <p>Click the following button to call the function</p>

        <form>
            <input type="button" onclick="sayHello()" value="Say
Hello">
        </form>

        <p>Use different text in write method and then try...</p>
    </body>
</html>
```

Output

Click the following button to call the function

Say Hello

Use different text in write method and then try...

Hello there!

Function Parameters

Till now, we have seen functions without parameters. But there is a facility to pass different parameters while calling a function. These passed parameters can be captured inside the function and any manipulation can be done over those parameters. A function can take multiple parameters separated by comma.

Example

Try the following example. We have modified our **sayHello** function here. Now it takes two parameters.

```
<html>
    <head>
        <script type="text/javascript">
            function sayHello(name, age)
            {
                document.write (name + " is " + age + " years
old.");
            }
        </script>

    </head>
    <body>
        <p>Click the following button to call the function</p>

        <form>
            <input type="button" onclick="sayHello('Zara', 7)"
value="Say Hello">
        </form>
        <p>Use different parameters inside the function and then
try...</p>
    </body>
</html>
```

Output

Click the following button to call the function

[Say Hello]

Use different parameters inside the function and then try...

Zara is 7 years old.

The return Statement

A JavaScript function can have an optional **return** statement. This is required if you want to return a value from a function. This statement should be the last statement in a function.

For example, you can pass two numbers in a function and then you can expect the function to return their multiplication in your calling program.

Example

Try the following example. It defines a function that takes two parameters and concatenates them before returning the resultant in the calling program.

```
<html>
    <head>

        <script type="text/javascript">
        function concatenate(first, last)
        {
            var full;
            full = first + last;
            return full;
        }

        function secondFunction()
        {
            var result;
            result = concatenate('Zara', 'Ali');
            document.write (result );
        }
        </script>

    </head>
```

93

```
<body>
    <p>Click the following button to call the function</p>

    <form>
        <input type="button" onclick="secondFunction()"
value="Call Function">
    <form>

    <p>Use different parameters inside the function and then
try...</p>

    </body>
</html>
```

Output

Click the following button to call the function

Call Function

Use different parameters inside the function and then try...

ZaraAli

There is a lot to learn about JavaScript functions, however we have covered the most important concepts in this tutorial.

- JavaScript Nested Functions
- JavaScript Function( ) Constructor
- JavaScript Function Literals

JavaScript – Events

What is an Event ?

JavaScript's interaction with HTML is handled through events that occur when the user or the browser manipulates a page.

When the page loads, it is called an event. When the user clicks a button, that click too is an event. Other examples include events like pressing any key, closing a window, resizing a window, etc.

Developers can use these events to execute JavaScript coded responses, which cause buttons to close windows, messages to be displayed to users, data to be validated, and virtually any other type of response imaginable.

Events are a part of the Document Object Model (DOM) Level 3 and every HTML element contains a set of events which can trigger JavaScript Code.

Please go through this small tutorial for a better understanding HTML Event Reference. Here we will see a few examples to understand a relation between Event and JavaScript –

onclick Event Type

This is the most frequently used event type which occurs when a user clicks the left button of his mouse. You can put your validation, warning etc., against this event type.

Example

Try the following example.

```
<html>
   <head>

      <script type="text/javascript">
         <!--
            function sayHello() {
               alert("Hello World")
            }
         //-->
      </script>

   </head>

   <body>
      <p>Click the following button and see result</p>

      <form>
         <input type="button" onclick="sayHello()" value="Say
Hello" />
      </form>

   </body>
</html>
```

Output

Click the following button and see result

[Say Hello]

www.tutorialspoint.com says: ✕

Hello World

[OK]

onsubmit Event type

onsubmit is an event that occurs when you try to submit a form. You can put your form validation against this event type.

Example

The following example shows how to use onsubmit. Here we are calling a **validate()** function before submitting a form data to the webserver. If **validate()** function returns true, the form will be submitted, otherwise it will not submit the data.

Try the following example.

```html
<html>
   <head>
      <script type="text/javascript">
         <!--
            function validation() {
               all validation goes here
               .........
               return either true or false
            }
         //-->
      </script>

   </head>
   <body>

      <form method="POST" action="t.cgi" onsubmit="return validate()">
         .......
         <input type="submit" value="Submit" />
      </form>

   </body>
</html>
```

onmouseover and onmouseout

These two event types will help you create nice effects with images or even with text as well. The **onmouseover** event triggers when you bring your mouse over any element and the **onmouseout** triggers when you move your mouse out from that element. Try the following example.

```html
<html>
   <head>

      <script type="text/javascript">
         <!--
            function over() {
               document.write ("Mouse Over");
            }

            function out() {
               document.write ("Mouse Out");
            }

         //-->
      </script>

   </head>
   <body>
      <p>Bring your mouse inside the division to see the
result:</p>

      <div onmouseover="over()" onmouseout="out()">
         <h2> This is inside the division </h2>
      </div>

   </body>
</html>
```

Output

Mouse Over

HTML 5 Standard Events

The standard HTML 5 events are listed here for your reference. Here script indicates a Javascript function to be executed against that event.

Attribute	Value	Description
Offline	script	Triggers when the document goes offline
Onabort	script	Triggers on an abort event
onafterprint	script	Triggers after the document is printed
onbeforeonload	script	Triggers before the document loads
onbeforeprint	script	Triggers before the document is printed
onblur	script	Triggers when the window loses focus

oncanplay	script	Triggers when media can start play, but might has to stop for buffering
oncanplaythrough	script	Triggers when media can be played to the end, without stopping for buffering
onchange	script	Triggers when an element changes
onclick	script	Triggers on a mouse click
oncontextmenu	script	Triggers when a context menu is triggered
ondblclick	script	Triggers on a mouse double-click
ondrag	script	Triggers when an element is dragged
ondragend	script	Triggers at the end of a drag operation

ondragenter	script	Triggers when an element has been dragged to a valid drop target
ondragleave	script	Triggers when an element is being dragged over a valid drop target
ondragover	script	Triggers at the start of a drag operation
ondragstart	script	Triggers at the start of a drag operation
ondrop	script	Triggers when dragged element is being dropped
ondurationchange	script	Triggers when the length of the media is changed
onemptied	script	Triggers when a media resource element suddenly becomes empty.
onended	script	Triggers when media has reach the end

onerror	script	Triggers when an error occur
onfocus	script	Triggers when the window gets focus
onformchange	script	Triggers when a form changes
onforminput	script	Triggers when a form gets user input
onhaschange	script	Triggers when the document has change
oninput	script	Triggers when an element gets user input
oninvalid	script	Triggers when an element is invalid
onkeydown	script	Triggers when a key is pressed

onkeypress	script	Triggers when a key is pressed and released
onkeyup	script	Triggers when a key is released
onload	script	Triggers when the document loads
onloadeddata	script	Triggers when media data is loaded
onloadedmetadata	script	Triggers when the duration and other media data of a media element is loaded
onloadstart	script	Triggers when the browser starts to load the media data
onmessage	script	Triggers when the message is triggered
onmousedown	script	Triggers when a mouse button is pressed

onmousemove	script	Triggers when the mouse pointer moves
onmouseout	script	Triggers when the mouse pointer moves out of an element
onmouseover	script	Triggers when the mouse pointer moves over an element
onmouseup	script	Triggers when a mouse button is released
onmousewheel	script	Triggers when the mouse wheel is being rotated
onoffline	script	Triggers when the document goes offline
onoine	script	Triggers when the document comes online
ononline	script	Triggers when the document comes online

onpagehide	script	Triggers when the window is hidden
onpageshow	script	Triggers when the window becomes visible
onpause	script	Triggers when media data is paused
onplay	script	Triggers when media data is going to start playing
onplaying	script	Triggers when media data has start playing
onpopstate	script	Triggers when the window's history changes
onprogress	script	Triggers when the browser is fetching the media data
onratechange	script	Triggers when the media data's playing rate has changed

onreadystatechange	script	Triggers when the ready-state changes
onredo	script	Triggers when the document performs a redo
onresize	script	Triggers when the window is resized
onscroll	script	Triggers when an element's scrollbar is being scrolled
onseeked	script	Triggers when a media element's seeking attribute is no longer true, and the seeking has ended
onseeking	script	Triggers when a media element's seeking attribute is true, and the seeking has begun
onselect	script	Triggers when an element is selected

onstalled	script	Triggers when there is an error in fetching media data
onstorage	script	Triggers when a document loads
onsubmit	script	Triggers when a form is submitted
onsuspend	script	Triggers when the browser has been fetching media data, but stopped before the entire media file was fetched
ontimeupdate	script	Triggers when media changes its playing position
onundo	script	Triggers when a document performs an undo
onunload	script	Triggers when the user leaves the document

onvolumechange	script	Triggers when media changes the volume, also when volume is set to "mute"
onwaiting	script	Triggers when media has stopped playing, but is expected to resume

JavaScript and Cookies

What are Cookies ?

Web Browsers and Servers use HTTP protocol to communicate and HTTP is a stateless protocol. But for a commercial website, it is required to maintain session information among different pages. For example, one user registration ends after completing many pages. But how to maintain users' session information across all the web pages.

In many situations, using cookies is the most efficient method of remembering and tracking preferences, purchases, commissions, and other information required for better visitor experience or site statistics.

How It Works ?

Your server sends some data to the visitor's browser in the form of a cookie. The browser may accept the cookie. If it does, it is stored as a plain text record on the visitor's hard drive. Now, when the visitor arrives at another page on your site, the browser sends the same cookie to the server for retrieval. Once retrieved, your server knows/remembers what was stored earlier.

Cookies are a plain text data record of 5 variable-length fields –

- **Expires** – The date the cookie will expire. If this is blank, the cookie will expire when the visitor quits the browser.
- **Domain** – The domain name of your site.
- **Path** – The path to the directory or web page that set the cookie. This may be blank if you want to retrieve the cookie from any directory or page.
- **Secure** – If this field contains the word "secure", then the cookie may only be retrieved with a secure server. If this field is blank, no such restriction exists.
- **Name=Value** – Cookies are set and retrieved in the form of key-value pairs

Cookies were originally designed for CGI programming. The data contained in a cookie is automatically transmitted between the web browser and the web server, so CGI scripts on the server can read and write cookie values that are stored on the client.

JavaScript can also manipulate cookies using the **cookie** property of the **Document** object. JavaScript can read, create, modify, and delete the cookies that apply to the current web page.

Storing Cookies

The simplest way to create a cookie is to assign a string value to the document.cookie object, which looks like this.

```
document.cookie = "key1=value1;key2=value2;expires=date";
```

Here the **expires** attribute is optional. If you provide this attribute with a valid date or time, then the cookie will expire on a given date or time and thereafter, the cookies' value will not be accessible.

Note – Cookie values may not include semicolons, commas, or whitespace. For this reason, you may want to use the JavaScript **escape()** function to encode the value before storing it in the cookie. If you do this, you will also have to use the corresponding **unescape()** function when you read the cookie value.

Example

Try the following. It sets a customer name in an input cookie.

```html
<html>
    <head>

        <script type="text/javascript">
            <!--
                function WriteCookie()
                {
                    if( document.myform.customer.value == "" ){
                        alert("Enter some value!");
                        return;
                    }
                    cookievalue=
```

113

```
escape(document.myform.customer.value) + ";";
            document.cookie="name=" + cookievalue;
            document.write ("Setting Cookies : " + "name=" +
cookievalue );
         }
      //-->
   </script>

   </head>

   <body>

      <form name="myform" action="">
         Enter name: <input type="text" name="customer"/>
         <input type="button" value="Set Cookie"
onclick="WriteCookie();"/>
      </form>

   </body>
</html>
```

Output

Now your machine has a cookie called **name**. You can set multiple cookies using multiple key=value pairs separated by comma.

Reading Cookies

Reading a cookie is just as simple as writing one, because the value of the document.cookie object is the cookie. So you can use this string whenever you want to access the cookie. The document.cookie string will keep a list of name=value pairs separated by semicolons, where **name** is the name of a cookie and value is its string value.

You can use strings' **split()** function to break a string into key and values as follows –

Example

Try the following example to get all the cookies.

```
<html>
    <head>

        <script type="text/javascript">
            <!--
            function ReadCookie()
            {
                var allcookies = document.cookie;
                document.write ("All Cookies : " + allcookies );

                // Get all the cookies pairs in an array
                cookiearray = allcookies.split(';');

                // Now take key value pair out of this array
                for(var i=0; i<cookiearray.length; i++){
                    name = cookiearray[i].split('=')[0];
                    value = cookiearray[i].split('=')[1];
                    document.write ("Key is : " + name + " and
Value is : " + value);
```

```
                }
              }
         //-->
      </script>

   </head>
   <body>

      <form name="myform" action="">
         <p> click the following button and see the result:</p>
         <input type="button" value="Get Cookie"
onclick="ReadCookie()"/>
      </form>

   </body>
</html>
```

Note – Here **length** is a method of **Array** class which returns the length of an array. We will discuss Arrays in a separate chapter. By that time, please try to digest it.

Note – There may be some other cookies already set on your machine.

The above code will display all the cookies set on your machine.

Setting Cookies Expiry Date

You can extend the life of a cookie beyond the current browser session by setting an expiration date and saving the expiry date within the cookie. This can be done by setting the **'expires'** attribute to a date and time.

Example

Try the following example. It illustrates how to extend the expiry date of a cookie by 1 Month.

```html
<html>
    <head>

        <script type="text/javascript">
            <!--
            function WriteCookie()
            {
                var now = new Date();
                now.setMonth( now.getMonth() + 1 );
                cookievalue =
escape(document.myform.customer.value) + ";"

                document.cookie="name=" + cookievalue;
                document.cookie = "expires=" + now.toUTCString()
+ ";"

                document.write ("Setting Cookies : " + "name=" +
cookievalue );
            }
            //-->
        </script>

    </head>
    <body>
```

```
    <form name="formname" action="">
        Enter name: <input type="text" name="customer"/>
        <input type="button" value="Set Cookie"
onclick="WriteCookie()"/>
    </form>

  </body>
</html>
```

Output

Enter name: [   ] Set Cookie

Deleting a Cookie

Sometimes you will want to delete a cookie so that subsequent attempts to read the cookie return nothing. To do this, you just need to set the expiry date to a time in the past.

Example

Try the following example. It illustrates how to delete a cookie by setting its expiry date to one month behind the current date.

```html
<html>
    <head>

        <script type="text/javascript">
            <!--
            function WriteCookie()
            {
                var now = new Date();
                now.setMonth( now.getMonth() - 1 );
                cookievalue =
escape(document.myform.customer.value) + ";"

                document.cookie="name=" + cookievalue;
                document.cookie = "expires=" + now.toUTCString()
+ ";"
                document.write("Setting Cookies : " + "name=" +
cookievalue );
            }
            //-->
        </script>

    </head>
    <body>

        <form name="formname" action="">
            Enter name: <input type="text" name="customer"/>
```

```
        <input type="button" value="Set Cookie"
onclick="WriteCookie()"/>
      </form>

    </body>
</html>
```

Output

Enter name: [   ] [Set Cookie]

JavaScript - Page Redirection

What is Page Redirection ?

You might have encountered a situation where you clicked a URL to reach a page X but internally you were directed to another page Y. It happens due to **page redirection**. This concept is different from JavaScript Page Refresh.

There could be various reasons why you would like to redirect a user from the original page. We are listing down a few of the reasons −

- You did not like the name of your domain and you are moving to a new one. In such a scenario, you may want to direct all your visitors to the new site. Here you can maintain your old domain but put a single page with a page redirection such that all your old domain visitors can come to your new domain.
- You have built-up various pages based on browser versions or their names or may be based on different countries, then instead of using your server-side page redirection, you can use client-side page redirection to land your users on the appropriate page.
- The Search Engines may have already indexed your pages. But while moving to another domain, you would not like to lose your visitors coming through search engines. So you can use client-side page redirection. But keep in mind this should not be done to fool the search engine, it could lead your site to get banned.

How Page Re-direction Works ?

The implementations of Page-Redirection are as follows.

Example 1

It is quite simple to do a page redirect using JavaScript at client side. To redirect your site visitors to a new page, you just need to add a line in your head section as follows.

```html
<html>
   <head>

      <script type="text/javascript">
         <!--
            function Redirect() {
               window.location="http://www.tutorialspoint.com";
            }
         //-->
      </script>

   </head>

   <body>
      <p>Click the following button, you will be redirected to
home page.</p>

      <form>
         <input type="button" value="Redirect Me"
onclick="Redirect();" />
      </form>

   </body>
</html>
```

Output

Click the following button, you will be redirected to home page.

| Redirect Me |

Example 2

You can show an appropriate message to your site visitors before redirecting them to a new page. This would need a bit time delay to load a new page. The following example shows how to implement the same. Here setTimeout() is a built-in JavaScript function which can be used to execute another function after a given time interval.

```
<html>
   <head>

      <script type="text/javascript">
         <!--
            function Redirect() {
               window.location="http://www.tutorialspoint.com";
            }

            document.write("You will be redirected to main page
in 10 sec.");
            setTimeout('Redirect()', 10000);
         //-->
      </script>

   </head>
```

```
        <body>
        </body>
</html>
```

Output

> You will be redirected to main page in 10 sec.

```
You will be redirected to tutorialspoint.com main page in 10 seconds!
```

Example 3

The following example shows how to redirect your site visitors onto a different page based on their browsers.

```
<html>
    <head>

        <script type="text/javascript">
            <!--
                var browsername=navigator.appName;
                if( browsername == "Netscape" )
                {

window.location="http://www.location.com/ns.htm";
                }
                else if ( browsername =="Microsoft Internet
Explorer")
                {

window.location="http://www.location.com/ie.htm";
```

```
            }
        else
        {

window.location="http://www.location.com/other.htm";
        }
        //-->
    </script>

    </head>

    <body>
    </body>
</html>
```

JavaScript - Dialog Boxes

JavaScript supports three important types of dialog boxes. These dialog boxes can be used to raise and alert, or to get confirmation on any input or to have a kind of input from the users. Here we will discuss each dialog box one by one.

Alert Dialog Box

An alert dialog box is mostly used to give a warning message to the users. For example, if one input field requires to enter some text but the user does not provide any input, then as a part of validation, you can use an alert box to give a warning message.

Nonetheless, an alert box can still be used for friendlier messages. Alert box gives only one button "OK" to select and proceed.

Example

```
<html>
    <head>
        <script type="text/javascript">
            <!--
                function Warn() {
                    alert ("This is a warning message!");
                    document.write ("This is a warning message!");
                }
            //-->
        </script>
    </head>
    <body>
        <p>Click the following button to see the result: </p>

        <form>
            <input type="button" value="Click Me"
onclick="Warn();" />
        </form>

    </body>
</html>
```

Output

Click the following button to see the result:

Click Me

This is a warning message!

OK

Confirmation Dialog Box

A confirmation dialog box is mostly used to take user's consent on any option. It displays a dialog box with two buttons: **Cancel**.

If the user clicks on the OK button, the window method **confirm()** will return true. If the user clicks on the Cancel button, then **confirm()** returns false. You can use a confirmation dialog box as follows.

Output

```html
<html>
   <head>

      <script type="text/javascript">
         <!--
            function getConfirmation(){
               var retVal = confirm("Do you want to continue ?");
               if( retVal == true ){
                  document.write ("User wants to continue!");
                  return true;
               }
               else{
                  Document.write ("User does not want to continue!");
                  return false;
               }
            }
         //-->
      </script>

   </head>
   <body>
```

129

```
    <p>Click the following button to see the result: </p>

    <form>
        <input type="button" value="Click Me"
onclick="getConfirmation();" />
    </form>

    </body>
</html>
```

Output

This is a warning message!

Prompt Dialog Box

The prompt dialog box is very useful when you want to pop-up a text box to get user input. Thus, it enables you to interact with the user. The user needs to fill in the field and then click OK.

This dialog box is displayed using a method called **prompt()** which takes two parameters: (i) a label which you want to display in the text box and (ii) a default string to display in the text box.

This dialog box has two buttons: **OK** and **Cancel**. If the user clicks the OK button, the window method **prompt()** will return the entered value from the text box. If the user clicks the Cancel button, the window method **prompt()**returns **null**.

Example

The following example shows how to use a prompt dialog box –

```html
<html>
   <head>

      <script type="text/javascript">
         <!--
            function getValue(){
               var retVal = prompt("Enter your name : ", "your
name here");
               document.write("You have entered : " + retVal);
            }
         //-->
      </script>

   </head>
```

131

```
<body>
    <p>Click the following button to see the result: </p>

    <form>
        <input type="button" value="Click Me"
onclick="getValue();" />
    </form>

    </body>
</html>
```

Output

Click the following button to see the result:

Click Me

Enter your name :

your name here

OK   Cancel

JavaScript - Void Keyword

void is an important keyword in JavaScript which can be used as a unary operator that appears before its single operand, which may be of any type. This operator specifies an expression to be evaluated without returning a value.

Syntax

The syntax of **void** can be either of the following two –

```
<head>

    <script type="text/javascript">
    <!--
        void func()
        javascript:void func()

        or:

        void(func())
        javascript:void(func())
    //-->
    </script>

</head>
```

Example 1

The most common use of this operator is in a client-side *javascript:* URL, where it allows you to evaluate an expression for its side-effects without the browser displaying the value of the evaluated expression.

Here the expression **alert ('Warning!!!')** is evaluated but it is not loaded back into the current document −

```
<html>
    <head>

        <script type="text/javascript">
            <!--
            //-->
        </script>

    </head>
    <body>

        <p>Click the following, This won't react at all...</p>
        <a href="javascript:void(alert('Warning!!!'))">Click
me!</a>

    </body>
</html>
```

Output

Click the following, This won't react at all...

Click me!

Warning!!!

OK

Example 2

Take a look at the following example. The following link does nothing because the expression "0" has no effect in JavaScript. Here the expression "0" is evaluated, but it is not loaded back into the current document.

```html
<html>
    <head>

        <script type="text/javascript">
            <!--
            //-->
        </script>

    </head>
    <body>
```

135

```
<p>Click the following, This won't react at all...</p>
<a href="javascript:void(0)">Click me!</a>

    </body>
</html>
```

Output

Click the following, This won't react at all...

Click me!

Example 3

Another use of **void** is to purposely generate the **undefined** value as follows.

```
<html>
    <head>

        <script type="text/javascript">
            <!--
                function getValue(){
                    var a,b,c;

                    a = void ( b = 5, c = 7 );
                    document.write('a = ' + a + ' b = ' + b +' c = '
+ c );
                }
            //-->
```

```html
    </script>

  </head>

  <body>
    <p>Click the following to see the result:</p>

    <form>
      <input type="button" value="Click Me"
onclick="getValue();" />
    </form>

  </body>
</html>
```

Output

Click the following to see the result:

[Click Me]

a = undefined b = 5 c = 7

JavaScript - Page Printing

Many times you would like to place a button on your webpage to print the content of that web page via an actual printer. JavaScript helps you to implement this functionality using the **print** function of **window** object.

The JavaScript print function **window.print()** prints the current web page when executed. You can call this function directly using the **onclick** event as shown in the following example.

Example

Try the following example.

```html
<html>
    <head>

        <script type="text/javascript">
            <!--
            //-->
        </script>

    </head>

    <body>

        <form>
            <input type="button" value="Print"
onclick="window.print()" />
        </form>

    </body>
<html>
```

Output

Although it serves the purpose of getting a printout, it is not a recommended way. A printer friendly page is really just a page with text, no images, graphics, or advertising.

You can make a page printer friendly in the following ways −

- Make a copy of the page and leave out unwanted text and graphics, then link to that printer friendly page from the original. Check Example.
- If you do not want to keep an extra copy of a page, then you can mark your printable text using proper comments like <!-- PRINT STARTS HERE -->..... <!-- PRINT ENDS HERE --> and then you can use PERL or any other script in the background to purge printable text and display for final printing. We at Tutorialspoint use this method to provide print facility to our site visitors. Check Example.

How to Print a Page

If you don't find the above facilities on a web page, then you can use the browser's standard toolbar to get print the web page. Follow the link as follows.

File → Print → Click OK button.

JavaScript - Objects Overview

JavaScript is an Object Oriented Programming (OOP) language. A programming language can be called object-oriented if it provides four basic capabilities to developers −

- **Encapsulation** − the capability to store related information, whether data or methods, together in an object.
- **Aggregation** − the capability to store one object inside another object.
- **Inheritance** − the capability of a class to rely upon another class (or number of classes) for some of its properties and methods.
- **Polymorphism** − the capability to write one function or method that works in a variety of different ways.

Objects are composed of attributes. If an attribute contains a function, it is considered to be a method of the object, otherwise the attribute is considered a property.

Object Properties

Object properties can be any of the three primitive data types, or any of the abstract data types, such as another object. Object properties are usually variables that are used internally in the object's methods, but can also be globally visible variables that are used throughout the page.

The syntax for adding a property to an object is −

```
objectName.objectProperty = propertyValue;
```

For example − The following code gets the document title using the **"title"**property of the **document** object.

```
var str = document.title;
```

Object Methods

Methods are the functions that let the object do something or let something be done to it. There is a small difference between a function and a method – at a function is a standalone unit of statements and a method is attached to an object and can be referenced by the **this** keyword.

Methods are useful for everything from displaying the contents of the object to the screen to performing complex mathematical operations on a group of local properties and parameters.

For example – Following is a simple example to show how to use the **write()** method of document object to write any content on the document.

```
document.write("This is test");
```

User-Defined Objects

All user-defined objects and built-in objects are descendants of an object called **Object**.

The new Operator

The **new** operator is used to create an instance of an object. To create an object, the **new** operator is followed by the constructor method.

In the following example, the constructor methods are Object(), Array(), and Date(). These constructors are built-in JavaScript functions.

```
var employee = new Object();
var books = new Array("C++", "Perl", "Java");
var day = new Date("August 15, 1947");
```

The Object() Constructor

A constructor is a function that creates and initializes an object. JavaScript provides a special constructor function called **Object()** to build the object. The return value of the **Object()** constructor is assigned to a variable.

The variable contains a reference to the new object. The properties assigned to the object are not variables and are not defined with the **var** keyword.

Example 1

Try the following example; it demonstrates how to create an Object.

```
<html>
   <head>
      <title>User-defined objects</title>
      <script type="text/javascript">
         var book = new Object();   // Create the object
         book.subject = "Perl"; // Assign properties to the
object
         book.author  = "Mohtashim";
      </script>
         </head>
      <body>
      <script type="text/javascript">
         document.write("Book name is : " + book.subject +
"<br>");
         document.write("Book author is : " + book.author +
"<br>");
      </script>

   </body>
</html>
```

Output

Example 2

This example demonstrates how to create an object with a User-Defined Function. Here **this** keyword is used to refer to the object that has been passed to a function.

```html
<html>
   <head>

   <title>User-defined objects</title>

      <script type="text/javascript">
         function book(title, author){
            this.title = title;
            this.author  = author;
         }
      </script>
   </head>
   <body>

      <script type="text/javascript">
         var myBook = new book("Perl", "Mohtashim");
         document.write("Book title is : " + myBook.title +
"<br>");
         document.write("Book author is : " + myBook.author +
"<br>");
      </script>

   </body>
</html>
```

Output

```
Book title is : Perl
Book author is : Mohtashim
```

Defining Methods for an Object

The previous examples demonstrate how the constructor creates the object and assigns properties. But we need to complete the definition of an object by assigning methods to it.

Example

Try the following example; it shows how to add a function along with an object.

```html
<html>
    <head>
    <title>User-defined objects</title>

        <script type="text/javascript">
            // Define a function which will work as a method
            function addPrice(amount){
                this.price = amount;
            }

            function book(title, author){
                this.title = title;
                this.author  = author;
                this.addPrice = addPrice; // Assign that method as
property.
            }
        </script>

    </head>
```

```
    <body>

        <script type="text/javascript">
            var myBook = new book("Perl", "Mohtashim");
            myBook.addPrice(100);

            document.write("Book title is : " + myBook.title +
"<br>");
            document.write("Book author is : " + myBook.author +
"<br>");
            document.write("Book price is : " + myBook.price +
"<br>");
        </script>

    </body>
</html>
```

Output

```
Book title is : Perl
Book author is : Mohtashim
Book price is : 100
```

The 'with' Keyword

The **'with'** keyword is used as a kind of shorthand for referencing an object's properties or methods.

The object specified as an argument to **with** becomes the default object for the duration of the block that follows. The properties and methods for the object can be used without naming the object.

Syntax

The syntax for with object is as follows −

```
with (object){
    properties used without the object name and dot
}
```

Example

Try the following example.

```
<html>
    <head>
    <title>User-defined objects</title>

        <script type="text/javascript">
            // Define a function which will work as a method
            function addPrice(amount){
                with(this){
                    price = amount;
                }
            }

            function book(title, author){
                this.title = title;
```

```
            this.author  = author;
            this.price = 0;
            this.addPrice = addPrice; // Assign that method as
property.
        }
    </script>

  </head>
  <body>

    <script type="text/javascript">
        var myBook = new book("Perl", "Mohtashim");
        myBook.addPrice(100);

        document.write("Book title is : " + myBook.title +
"<br>");
        document.write("Book author is : " + myBook.author +
"<br>");
        document.write("Book price is : " + myBook.price +
"<br>");
    </script>

  </body>
</html>
```

Output

```
Book title is : Perl
Book author is : Mohtashim
Book price is : 100
```

JavaScript Native Objects

JavaScript has several built-in or native objects. These objects are accessible anywhere in your program and will work the same way in any browser running in any operating system.

Here is the list of all important JavaScript Native Objects –

- JavaScript Number Object
- JavaScript Boolean Object
- JavaScript String Object
- JavaScript Array Object
- JavaScript Date Object
- JavaScript Math Object
- JavaScript RegExp Object

JavaScript - The Number Object

The **Number** object represents numerical date, either integers or floating-point numbers. In general, you do not need to worry about **Number** objects because the browser automatically converts number literals to instances of the number class.

Syntax

The syntax for creating a **number** object is as follows –

```
var val = new Number(number);
```

In the place of number, if you provide any non-number argument, then the argument cannot be converted into a number, it returns **NaN** (Not-a-Number).

Number Properties

Here is a list of each property and their description.

Property	Description
MAX_VALUE	The largest possible value a number in JavaScript can have 1.79769313486231 57E+308
MIN_VALUE	The smallest possible value a number in JavaScript can have 5E-324
NaN	Equal to a value that is not a number.
NEGATIVE_INFINITY	A value that is less than MIN_VALUE.
POSITIVE_INFINITY	A value that is greater than MAX_VALUE

prototype	A static property of the Number object. Use the prototype property to assign new properties and methods to the Number object in the current document
constructor	Returns the function that created this object's instance. By default this is the Number object.

In the following sections, we will take a few examples to demonstrate the properties of Number.

Number Methods

The Number object contains only the default methods that are a part of every object's definition.

Method	Description
toExponential()	Forces a number to display in exponential notation, even if the number is in the range in which JavaScript normally uses standard notation.
toFixed()	Formats a number with a specific number of digits to the right of the decimal.
toLocaleString()	Returns a string value version of the current number in a format that may vary according to a browser's local settings.
toPrecision()	Defines how many total digits (including digits to the left and right of the decimal) to display of a number.

toString()	Returns the string representation of the number's value.
valueOf()	Returns the number's value.

In the following sections, we will have a few examples to explain the methods of Number.

JavaScript - The Boolean Object

The **Boolean** object represents two values, either "true" or "false". If *value*parameter is omitted or is 0, -0, null, false, **NaN,** undefined, or the empty string (""), the object has an initial value of false.

Syntax

Use the following syntax to create a **boolean** object.

```
var val = new Boolean(value);
```

Boolean Properties

Here is a list of the properties of Boolean object –

Property	Description
constructor	Returns a reference to the Boolean function that created the object.
prototype	The prototype property allows you to add properties and methods to an object.

In the following sections, we will have a few examples to illustrate the properties of Boolean object.

157

Boolean Methods

Here is a list of the methods of Boolean object and their description.

Method	Description
toSource()	Returns a string containing the source of the Boolean object; you can use this string to create an equivalent object.
toString()	Returns a string of either "true" or "false" depending upon the value of the object.
valueOf()	Returns the primitive value of the Boolean object.

In the following sections, we will have a few examples to demonstrate the usage of the Boolean methods.

JavaScript - The Strings Object

The **String** object lets you work with a series of characters; it wraps Javascript's string primitive data type with a number of helper methods.

As JavaScript automatically converts between string primitives and String objects, you can call any of the helper methods of the String object on a string primitive.

Syntax

Use the following syntax to create a String object –

```
var val = new String(string);
```

The **String** parameter is a series of characters that has been properly encoded.

String Properties

Here is a list of the properties of String object and their description.

Property	Description
constructor	Returns a reference to the String function that created the object.
length	Returns the length of the string.
prototype	The prototype property allows you to add properties and methods to an object.

In the following sections, we will have a few examples to demonstrate the usage of String properties.

String Methods

Here is a list of the methods available in String object along with their description.

Method	Description
charAt()	Returns the character at the specified index.
charCodeAt()	Returns a number indicating the Unicode value of the character at the given index.
concat()	Combines the text of two strings and returns a new string.
indexOf()	Returns the index within the calling String object of the first occurrence of the specified value, or -1 if not found.
lastIndexOf()	Returns the index within the calling String object of the last occurrence of the

	specified value, or -1 if not found.
localeCompare()	Returns a number indicating whether a reference string comes before or after or is the same as the given string in sort order.
match()	Used to match a regular expression against a string.
replace()	Used to find a match between a regular expression and a string, and to replace the matched substring with a new substring.
search()	Executes the search for a match between a regular expression and a specified string.

slice()	Extracts a section of a string and returns a new string.
split()	Splits a String object into an array of strings by separating the string into substrings.
substr()	Returns the characters in a string beginning at the specified location through the specified number of characters.
substring()	Returns the characters in a string between two indexes into the string.
toLocaleLowerCase()	The characters within a string are converted to lower case while respecting the current locale.
toLocaleUpperCase()	The characters within a string are converted to upper case while

	respecting the current locale.
toLowerCase()	Returns the calling string value converted to lower case.
toString()	Returns a string representing the specified object.
toUpperCase()	Returns the calling string value converted to uppercase.
valueOf()	Returns the primitive value of the specified object.

String HTML Wrappers

Here is a list of the methods that return a copy of the string wrapped inside an appropriate HTML tag.

Method	Description
anchor()	Creates an HTML anchor that is used as a hypertext target.
big()	Creates a string to be displayed in a big font as if it were in a <big> tag.
blink()	Creates a string to blink as if it were in a <blink> tag.
bold()	Creates a string to be displayed as bold as if it were in a <b> tag.
fixed()	Causes a string to be displayed in fixed-pitch font as if it were in a <tt> tag
fontcolor()	Causes a string to be displayed in the specified color as if it were in a <font color="color"> tag.

fontsize()	Causes a string to be displayed in the specified font size as if it were in a <font size="size"> tag.
italics()	Causes a string to be italic, as if it were in an <i> tag.
link()	Creates an HTML hypertext link that requests another URL.
small()	Causes a string to be displayed in a small font, as if it were in a <small> tag.
strike()	Causes a string to be displayed as struck-out text, as if it were in a <strike> tag.
sub()	Causes a string to be displayed as a subscript, as if it were in a <sub> tag
sup()	Causes a string to be displayed as a superscript, as if it were in a <sup> tag

In the following sections, we will have a few examples to demonstrate the usage of String methods.

JavaScript - The Arrays Object

The **Array** object lets you store multiple values in a single variable. It stores a fixed-size sequential collection of elements of the same type. An array is used to store a collection of data, but it is often more useful to think of an array as a collection of variables of the same type.

Syntax

Use the following syntax to create an **Array** object –

```
var fruits = new Array( "apple", "orange", "mango" );
```

The **Array** parameter is a list of strings or integers. When you specify a single numeric parameter with the Array constructor, you specify the initial length of the array. The maximum length allowed for an array is 4,294,967,295.

You can create array by simply assigning values as follows –

```
var fruits = [ "apple", "orange", "mango" ];
```

You will use ordinal numbers to access and to set values inside an array as follows.

```
fruits[0] is the first element
fruits[1] is the second element
fruits[2] is the third element
```

Array Properties

Here is a list of the properties of the Array object along with their description.

Property	Description
constructor	Returns a reference to the array function that created the object.
index	The property represents the zero-based index of the match in the string
input	This property is only present in arrays created by regular expression matches.
length	Reflects the number of elements in an array.
prototype	The prototype property allows you to add properties and methods to an object.

In the following sections, we will have a few examples to illustrate the usage of Array properties.

Array Methods

Here is a list of the methods of the Array object along with their description.

Method	Description
concat()	Returns a new array comprised of this array joined with other array(s) and/or value(s).
every()	Returns true if every element in this array satisfies the provided testing function.
filter()	Creates a new array with all of the elements of this array for which the provided filtering function returns true.
forEach()	Calls a function for each element in the array.
indexOf()	Returns the first (least) index of an element within the array equal to the specified value, or -1 if none is found.

join()	Joins all elements of an array into a string.
lastIndexOf()	Returns the last (greatest) index of an element within the array equal to the specified value, or -1 if none is found.
map()	Creates a new array with the results of calling a provided function on every element in this array.
pop()	Removes the last element from an array and returns that element.
push()	Adds one or more elements to the end of an array and returns the new length of the array.
reduce()	Apply a function simultaneously against two values of the array (from left-to-right) as to reduce it to a single value.
reduceRight()	Apply a function simultaneously against two values of the array

	(from right-to-left) as to reduce it to a single value.
reverse()	Reverses the order of the elements of an array -- the first becomes the last, and the last becomes the first.
shift()	Removes the first element from an array and returns that element.
slice()	Extracts a section of an array and returns a new array.
some()	Returns true if at least one element in this array satisfies the provided testing function.
toSource()	Represents the source code of an object
sort()	Sorts the elements of an array
splice()	Adds and/or removes elements from an array.

toString()	Returns a string representing the array and its elements.
unshift()	Adds one or more elements to the front of an array and returns the new length of the array.

In the following sections, we will have a few examples to demonstrate the usage of Array methods.

JavaScript - The Date Object

The Date object is a datatype built into the JavaScript language. Date objects are created with the **new Date( )** as shown below.

Once a Date object is created, a number of methods allow you to operate on it. Most methods simply allow you to get and set the year, month, day, hour, minute, second, and millisecond fields of the object, using either local time or UTC (universal, or GMT) time.

The ECMAScript standard requires the Date object to be able to represent any date and time, to millisecond precision, within 100 million days before or after 1/1/1970. This is a range of plus or minus 273,785 years, so JavaScript can represent date and time till the year 275755.

Syntax

You can use any of the following syntaxes to create a Date object using Date() constructor.

```
new Date( )
new Date(milliseconds)
new Date(datestring)
new Date(year,month,date[,hour,minute,second,millisecond ])
```

Note – Parameters in the brackets are always optional.

Here is a description of the parameters –

- **No Argument** – With no arguments, the Date() constructor creates a Date object set to the current date and time.

- **milliseconds** – When one numeric argument is passed, it is taken as the internal numeric representation of the date in milliseconds, as returned by the getTime() method. For example, passing the argument 5000 creates a date that represents five seconds past midnight on 1/1/70.
- **datestring** – When one string argument is passed, it is a string representation of a date, in the format accepted by the **Date.parse()**method.
- **7 agruments** – To use the last form of the constructor shown above. Here is a description of each argument:
    - **year** – Integer value representing the year. For compatibility (in order to avoid the Y2K problem), you should always specify the year in full; use 1998, rather than 98.
    - **month** – Integer value representing the month, beginning with 0 for January to 11 for December.
    - **date** – Integer value representing the day of the month.
    - **hour** – Integer value representing the hour of the day (24-hour scale).
    - **minute** – Integer value representing the minute segment of a time reading.
    - **second** – Integer value representing the second segment of a time reading.
    - **millisecond** – Integer value representing the millisecond segment of a time reading.

Date Properties

Here is a list of the properties of the Date object along with their description.

Property	Description
constructor	Specifies the function that creates an object's prototype.
prototype	The prototype property allows you to add properties and methods to an object

In the following sections, we will have a few examples to demonstrate the usage of different Date properties.

Date Methods

Here is a list of the methods used with **Date** and their description.

Method	Description
Date()	Returns today's date and time
getDate()	Returns the day of the month for the specified date according to local time.
getDay()	Returns the day of the week for the specified date according to local time.
getFullYear()	Returns the year of the specified date according to local time.
getHours()	Returns the hour in the specified date according to local time.

getMilliseconds()	Returns the milliseconds in the specified date according to local time.
getMinutes()	Returns the minutes in the specified date according to local time.
getMonth()	Returns the month in the specified date according to local time.
getSeconds()	Returns the seconds in the specified date according to local time.
getTime()	Returns the numeric value of the specified date as the number of milliseconds since January 1, 1970, 00:00:00 UTC.
getTimezoneOffset()	Returns the time-zone offset in minutes for the current locale.

getUTCDate()	Returns the day (date) of the month in the specified date according to universal time.
getUTCDay()	Returns the day of the week in the specified date according to universal time.
getUTCFullYear()	Returns the year in the specified date according to universal time.
getUTCHours()	Returns the hours in the specified date according to universal time.
getUTCMilliseconds()	Returns the milliseconds in the specified date according to universal time.
getUTCMinutes()	Returns the minutes in the specified date according to universal time.

getUTCMonth()	Returns the month in the specified date according to universal time.
getUTCSeconds()	Returns the seconds in the specified date according to universal time.
getYear()	**Deprecated** - Returns the year in the specified date according to local time. Use getFullYear instead.
setDate()	Sets the day of the month for a specified date according to local time.
setFullYear()	Sets the full year for a specified date according to local time.

setHours()	Sets the hours for a specified date according to local time.
setMilliseconds()	Sets the milliseconds for a specified date according to local time.
setMinutes()	Sets the minutes for a specified date according to local time.
setMonth()	Sets the month for a specified date according to local time.
setSeconds()	Sets the seconds for a specified date according to local time.
setTime()	Sets the Date object to the time represented by a number of milliseconds since January 1, 1970, 00:00:00 UTC.

setUTCDate()	Sets the day of the month for a specified date according to universal time.
setUTCFullYear()	Sets the full year for a specified date according to universal time.
setUTCHours()	Sets the hour for a specified date according to universal time.
setUTCMilliseconds()	Sets the milliseconds for a specified date according to universal time.
setUTCMinutes()	Sets the minutes for a specified date according to universal time.
setUTCMonth()	Sets the month for a specified date according to universal time.

setUTCSeconds()	Sets the seconds for a specified date according to universal time.
setYear()	**Deprecated -** Sets the year for a specified date according to local time. Use setFullYear instead.
toDateString()	Returns the "date" portion of the Date as a human-readable string.
toGMTString()	**Deprecated -** Converts a date to a string, using the Internet GMT conventions. Use toUTCString instead.
toLocaleDateString()	Returns the "date" portion of the Date as a string, using the current locale's conventions.
toLocaleFormat()	Converts a date to a string, using a format string.

toLocaleString()	Converts a date to a string, using the current locale's conventions.
toLocaleTimeString()	Returns the "time" portion of the Date as a string, using the current locale's conventions.
toSource()	Returns a string representing the source for an equivalent Date object; you can use this value to create a new object.
toString()	Returns a string representing the specified Date object.
toTimeString()	Returns the "time" portion of the Date as a human-readable string.
toUTCString()	Converts a date to a string, using the

	universal time convention.
valueOf()	Returns the primitive value of a Date object.

Converts a date to a string, using the universal time convention.

Date Static Methods

In addition to the many instance methods listed previously, the Date object also defines two static methods. These methods are invoked through the Date() constructor itself.

Method	Description
Date.parse( )	Parses a string representation of a date and time and returns the internal millisecond representation of that date.
Date.UTC( )	Returns the millisecond representation of the specified UTC date and time.

In the following sections, we will have a few examples to demonstrate the usages of Date Static methods.

JavaScript - The Math Object

The **math** object provides you properties and methods for mathematical constants and functions. Unlike other global objects, **Math** is not a constructor. All the properties and methods of **Math** are static and can be called by using Math as an object without creating it.

Thus, you refer to the constant **pi** as **Math.PI** and you call the *sine* function as **Math.sin(x)**, where x is the method's argument.

Syntax

The syntax to call the properties and methods of Math are as follows

```
var pi_val = Math.PI;
var sine_val = Math.sin(30);
```

Math Properties

Here is a list of all the properties of Math and their description.

Property	Description
**E **	Euler's constant and the base of natural logarithms, approximately 2.718.
LN2	Natural logarithm of 2, approximately 0.693.
LN10	Natural logarithm of 10, approximately 2.302.
LOG2E	Base 2 logarithm of E, approximately 1.442.
LOG10E	Base 10 logarithm of E, approximately 0.434.
PI	Ratio of the circumference of a circle to its diameter, approximately 3.14159.

SQRT1_2	Square root of 1/2; equivalently, 1 over the square root of 2, approximately 0.707.
SQRT2	Square root of 2, approximately 1.414.

In the following sections, we will have a few examples to demonstrate the usage of Math properties.

Math Methods

Here is a list of the methods associated with Math object and their description

Method	Description
abs()	Returns the absolute value of a number.
acos()	Returns the arccosine (in radians) of a number.
asin()	Returns the arcsine (in radians) of a number.
atan()	Returns the arctangent (in radians) of a number.
atan2()	Returns the arctangent of the quotient of its arguments.
ceil()	Returns the smallest integer greater than or equal to a number.
cos()	Returns the cosine of a number.

exp()	Returns E^N, where N is the argument, and E is Euler's constant, the base of the natural logarithm.
floor()	Returns the largest integer less than or equal to a number.
log()	Returns the natural logarithm (base E) of a number.
max()	Returns the largest of zero or more numbers.
min()	Returns the smallest of zero or more numbers.
pow()	Returns base to the exponent power, that is, base exponent.
random()	Returns a pseudo-random number between 0 and 1.
round()	Returns the value of a number rounded to the nearest integer.

sin()	Returns the sine of a number.
sqrt()	Returns the square root of a number.
tan()	Returns the tangent of a number.
toSource()	Returns the string "Math".

In the following sections, we will have a few examples to demonstrate the usage of the methods associated with Math.

Regular Expressions and RegExp Object

A regular expression is an object that describes a pattern of characters.

The JavaScript **RegExp** class represents regular expressions, and both String and **RegExp** define methods that use regular expressions to perform powerful pattern-matching and search-and-replace functions on text.

Syntax

A regular expression could be defined with the **RegExp ()** constructor, as follows −

```
var pattern = new RegExp(pattern, attributes);
```

or simply

```
var pattern = /pattern/attributes;
```

Here is the description of the parameters −

- **pattern** − A string that specifies the pattern of the regular expression or another regular expression.

- **attributes** − An optional string containing any of the "g", "i", and "m" attributes that specify global, case-insensitive, and multiline matches, respectively.

Brackets

Brackets ([]) have a special meaning when used in the context of regular expressions. They are used to find a range of characters.

Expression	Description
[...]	Any one character between the brackets.
[^...]	Any one character not between the brackets.
[0-9]	It matches any decimal digit from 0 through 9.
[a-z]	It matches any character from lowercase a through lowercase z.
[A-Z]	It matches any character from uppercase A through uppercase Z.
[a-Z]	It matches any character from lowercase a through uppercase Z.

The ranges shown above are general; you could also use the range [0-3] to match any decimal digit ranging from 0 through

3, or the range [b-v] to match any lowercase character ranging from **b** through **v**.

Quantifiers

The frequency or position of bracketed character sequences and single characters can be denoted by a special character. Each special character has a specific connotation. The +, *, ?, and $ flags all follow a character sequence.

Expression	Description
p+	It matches any string containing at least one p.
p*	It matches any string containing zero or more p's.
p?	It matches any string containing one or more p's.
p{**N**}	It matches any string containing a sequence of **N** p's
p{2,3}	It matches any string containing a sequence of two or three p's.

p{2, }	It matches any string containing a sequence of at least two p's.
p$	It matches any string with p at the end of it.
^p	It matches any string with p at the beginning of it.

Examples

Following examples explain more about matching characters.

Expression	Description
[^a-zA-Z]	It matches any string not containing any of the characters ranging from **a** through **z** and **A** through Z.
p.p	It matches any string containing **p,** followed by any character, in turn followed by another **p**.
^.{2}$	It matches any string containing exactly two characters.

<b>(.*)</b>	It matches any string enclosed within <b> and </b>.
p(hp)*	It matches any string containing a **p** followed by zero or more instances of the sequence **hp**.

Literal characters

Character	Description
Alphanumeric	Itself
\0	The NUL character (\u0000)
\t	Tab (\u0009)
\n	Newline (\u000A)
\v	Vertical tab (\u000B)

\f	Form feed (\u000C)
\r	Carriage return (\u000D)
\xnn	The Latin character specified by the hexadecimal number nn; for example, \x0A is the same as \n
\uxxxx	The Unicode character specified by the hexadecimal number xxxx; for example, \u0009 is the same as \t
\cX	The control character ^X; for example, \cJ is equivalent to the newline character \n

Metacharacters

A metacharacter is simply an alphabetical character preceded by a backslash that acts to give the combination a special meaning.

For instance, you can search for a large sum of money using the '\d' metacharacter: **/([\d]+)000/**, Here **\d** will search for any string of numerical character.

The following table lists a set of metacharacters which can be used in PERL Style Regular Expressions.

Character	Description
.	a single character
\s	a whitespace character (space, tab, newline)
\S	non-whitespace character
\d	a digit (0-9)
\D	a non-digit
\w	a word character (a-z, A-Z, 0-9, _)
\W	a non-word character
[\b]	a literal backspace (special case).
[aeiou]	matches a single character in the given set

[^aeiou]	matches a single character outside the given set
(foo|bar|baz)	matches any of the alternatives specified

Modifiers

Several modifiers are available that can simplify the way you work with **regexps,** like case sensitivity, searching in multiple lines, etc.

Modifier	Description
i	Perform case-insensitive matching.
m	Specifies that if the string has newline or carriage return characters, the ^ and $ operators will now match against a newline boundary, instead of a string boundary
g	Performs a global matchthat is, find all matches rather than stopping after the first match.

RegExp Properties

Here is a list of the properties associated with RegExp and their description.

Property	Description
constructor	Specifies the function that creates an object's prototype.
global	Specifies if the "g" modifier is set.
ignoreCase	Specifies if the "i" modifier is set.
lastIndex	The index at which to start the next match.
multiline	Specifies if the "m" modifier is set.
source	The text of the pattern.

In the following sections, we will have a few examples to demonstrate the usage of RegExp properties.

RegExp Methods

Here is a list of the methods associated with RegExp along with their description.

Method	Description
exec()	Executes a search for a match in its string parameter.
test()	Tests for a match in its string parameter.
toSource()	Returns an object literal representing the specified object; you can use this value to create a new object.
toString()	Returns a string representing the specified object.

In the following sections, we will have a few examples to demonstrate the usage of RegExp methods.

JavaScript - Document Object Model or DOM

Every web page resides inside a browser window which can be considered as an object.

A Document object represents the HTML document that is displayed in that window. The Document object has various properties that refer to other objects which allow access to and modification of document content.

The way a document content is accessed and modified is called the **Document Object Model**, or **DOM**. The Objects are organized in a hierarchy. This hierarchical structure applies to the organization of objects in a Web document.

- **Window object** – Top of the hierarchy. It is the outmost element of the object hierarchy.

- **Document object** – Each HTML document that gets loaded into a window becomes a document object. The document contains the contents of the page.

- **Form object** – Everything enclosed in the <form>...</form> tags sets the form object.

- **Form control elements** – The form object contains all the elements defined for that object such as text fields, buttons, radio buttons, and checkboxes.

Here is a simple hierarchy of a few important objects –

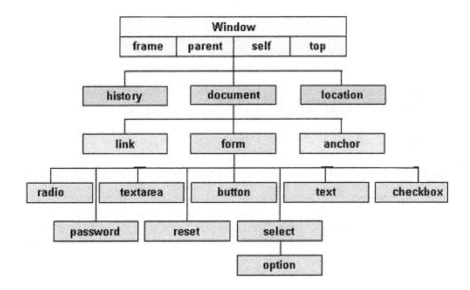

There are several DOMs in existence. The following sections explain each of these DOMs in detail and describe how you can use them to access and modify document content.

- The Legacy DOM – This is the model which was introduced in early versions of JavaScript language. It is well supported by all browsers, but allows access only to certain key portions of documents, such as forms, form elements, and images.

- The W3C DOM – This document object model allows access and modification of all document content and is standardized by the World Wide Web Consortium (W3C). This model is supported by almost all the modern browsers.

- The IE4 DOM – This document object model was introduced in Version 4 of Microsoft's Internet Explorer browser. IE 5 and later versions include support for most basic W3C DOM features.

DOM compatibility

If you want to write a script with the flexibility to use either W3C DOM or IE 4 DOM depending on their availability, then you can use a capability-testing approach that first checks for the existence of a method or property to determine whether the browser has the capability you desire. For example –

```
if (document.getElementById) {
    // If the W3C method exists, use it
}

else if (document.all) {
    // If the all[] array exists, use it
}

else {
    // Otherwise use the legacy DOM
}
```

JavaScript - Errors & Exceptions Handling

There are three types of errors in programming: (a) Syntax Errors, (b) Runtime Errors, and (c) Logical Errors.

Syntax Errors

Syntax errors, also called **parsing errors,** occur at compile time in traditional programming languages and at interpret time in JavaScript.

For example, the following line causes a syntax error because it is missing a closing parenthesis.

```
<script type="text/javascript">
    <!--
        window.print(;
    //-->
</script>
```

When a syntax error occurs in JavaScript, only the code contained within the same thread as the syntax error is affected and the rest of the code in other threads gets executed assuming nothing in them depends on the code containing the error.

Runtime Errors

Runtime errors, also called **exceptions,** occur during execution (after compilation/interpretation).

For example, the following line causes a runtime error because here the syntax is correct, but at runtime, it is trying to call a method that does not exist.

```
<script type="text/javascript">
    <!--
       window.printme();
    //-->
</script>
```

Exceptions also affect the thread in which they occur, allowing other JavaScript threads to continue normal execution.

Logical Errors

Logic errors can be the most difficult type of errors to track down. These errors are not the result of a syntax or runtime error. Instead, they occur when you make a mistake in the logic that drives your script and you do not get the result you expected.

You cannot catch those errors, because it depends on your business requirement what type of logic you want to put in your program.

The try...catch...finally Statement

The latest versions of JavaScript added exception handling capabilities. JavaScript implements the **try...catch...finally** construct as well as the **throw** operator to handle exceptions.

You can **catch** programmer-generated and **runtime** exceptions, but you cannot **catch** JavaScript syntax errors.

Here is the **try...catch...finally** block syntax –

```
<script type="text/javascript">
    <!--
        try {
            // Code to run
            [break;]
        }

        catch ( e ) {
            // Code to run if an exception occurs
            [break;]
        }

        [ finally {
            // Code that is always executed regardless of
            // an exception occurring
        }]
    //-->
</script>
```

The **try** block must be followed by either exactly one **catch** block or one **finally** block (or one of both). When an exception occurs in the **try** block, the exception is placed in **e** and the

catch block is executed. The optional **finally** block executes unconditionally after try/catch.

Examples

Here is an example where we are trying to call a non-existing function which in turn is raising an exception. Let us see how it behaves without **try...catch**–

```html
<html>
    <head>

        <script type="text/javascript">
        <!--
            function myFunc()
            {
                var a = 100;
                alert("Value of variable a is : " + a );
            }
        //-->
        </script>

    </head>

    <body>
        <p>Click the following to see the result:</p>

        <form>
            <input type="button" value="Click Me"
onclick="myFunc();" />
        </form>

    </body>
</html>
```

Now let us try to catch this exception using **try...catch** and display a user-friendly message. You can also suppress this message, if you want to hide this error from a user.

```html
<html>

   <head>

      <script type="text/javascript">
         <!--
            function myFunc()
            {
               var a = 100;
               try {
                  alert("Value of variable a is : " + a );
               }

               catch ( e ) {
                  alert("Error: " + e.description );
               }
            }
         //-->
      </script>

   </head>

   <body>
      <p>Click the following to see the result:</p>

      <form>
         <input type="button" value="Click Me"
onclick="myFunc();" />
      </form>

   </body>
</html>
```

You can use **finally** block which will always execute unconditionally after the try/catch. Here is an example.

```html
<html>

    <head>

        <script type="text/javascript">
            <!--
                function myFunc()
                {
                    var a = 100;

                    try {
                        alert("Value of variable a is : " + a );
                    }

                    catch ( e ) {
                        alert("Error: " + e.description );
                    }

                    finally {
                        alert("Finally block will always execute!" );
                    }
                }
            //-->
        </script>

    </head>

    <body>
        <p>Click the following to see the result:</p>

        <form>
            <input type="button" value="Click Me"
onclick="myFunc();" />
        </form>
```

```
    </body>
</html>
```

Output

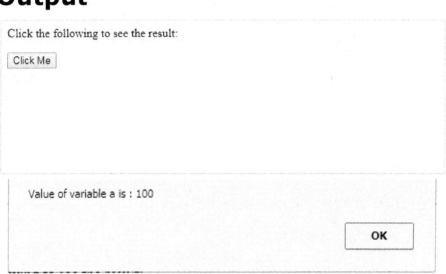

The throw Statement

You can use **throw** statement to raise your built-in exceptions or your customized exceptions. Later these exceptions can be captured and you can take an appropriate action.

Example

The following example demonstrates how to use a **throw** statement.

```
<html>

    <head>

        <script type="text/javascript">
            <!--
                function myFunc()
                {
                    var a = 100;
                    var b = 0;

                    try{
                        if ( b == 0 ){
                            throw( "Divide by zero error." );
                        }

                        else
                        {
                            var c = a / b;
                        }
                    }

                    catch ( e ) {
                        alert("Error: " + e );
                    }
                }
```

```
        //-->
    </script>

  </head>

  <body>
    <p>Click the following to see the result:</p>

    <form>
      <input type="button" value="Click Me"
onclick="myFunc();" />
    </form>

  </body>
</html>
```

Output

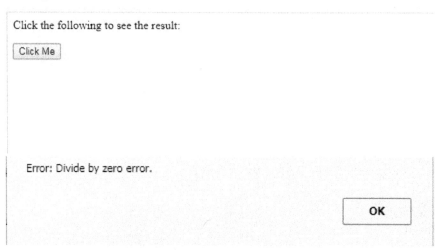

You can raise an exception in one function using a string, integer, Boolean, or an object and then you can capture that exception either in the same function as we did above, or in another function using a **try...catch** block.

The onerror() Method

The **onerror** event handler was the first feature to facilitate error handling in JavaScript. The **error** event is fired on the window object whenever an exception occurs on the page.

```html
<html>

    <head>

        <script type="text/javascript">
            <!--
                window.onerror = function () {
                    alert("An error occurred.");
                }
            //-->
        </script>

    </head>

    <body>
        <p>Click the following to see the result:</p>

        <form>
            <input type="button" value="Click Me"
onclick="myFunc();" />
        </form>

    </body>
</html>
```

Output

The **onerror** event handler provides three pieces of information to

identify the exact nature of the error −

215

- **Error message** – The same message that the browser would display for the given error
- **URL** – The file in which the error occurred
- **Line number**– The line number in the given URL that caused the error

Here is the example to show how to extract this information.

Example

```html
<html>

   <head>

      <script type="text/javascript">
         <!--
            window.onerror = function (msg, url, line) {
               alert("Message : " + msg );
               alert("url : " + url );
               alert("Line number : " + line );
            }
         //-->
      </script>

   </head>

   <body>
      <p>Click the following to see the result:</p>

      <form>
         <input type="button" value="Click Me"
onclick="myFunc();" />
      </form>
```

```
    </body>
</html>
```

Output

You can display extracted information in whatever way you think it is better.

You can use an **onerror** method, as shown below, to display an error message in case there is any problem in loading an image.

```
<img src="myimage.gif" onerror="alert('An error occurred
loading the image.')" />
```

You can use **onerror** with many HTML tags to display appropriate messages in case of errors.

JavaScript - Form Validation

Form validation normally used to occur at the server, after the client had entered all the necessary data and then pressed the Submit button. If the data entered by a client was incorrect or was simply missing, the server would have to send all the data back to the client and request that the form be resubmitted with correct information. This was really a lengthy process which used to put a lot of burden on the server.

JavaScript provides a way to validate form's data on the client's computer before sending it to the web server. Form validation generally performs two functions.

- **Basic Validation** – First of all, the form must be checked to make sure all the mandatory fields are filled in. It would require just a loop through each field in the form and check for data.

- **Data Format Validation** – Secondly, the data that is entered must be checked for correct form and value. Your code must include appropriate logic to test correctness of data.

Example

We will take an example to understand the process of validation. Here is a simple form in html format.

```
<html>

   <head>
      <title>Form Validation</title>

      <script type="text/javascript">
```

```
        <!--
        // Form validation code will come here.
        //-->
    </script>

</head>

<body>
    <form action="/cgi-bin/test.cgi" name="myForm"
onsubmit="return(validate());">
        <table cellspacing="2" cellpadding="2" border="1">

            <tr>
            <td align="right">Name</td>
            <td><input type="text" name="Name" /></td>
            </tr>

            <tr>
            <td align="right">EMail</td>
            <td><input type="text" name="EMail" /></td>
            </tr>

            <tr>
            <td align="right">Zip Code</td>
            <td><input type="text" name="Zip" /></td>
            </tr>

            <tr>
            <td align="right">Country</td>
            <td>
                <select name="Country">
                    <option value="-1" selected>[choose
yours]</option>
                    <option value="1">USA</option>
                    <option value="2">UK</option>
                    <option value="3">INDIA</option>
                </select>
```

```
                </td>
            </tr>

            <tr>
                <td align="right"></td>
                <td><input type="submit" value="Submit" /></td>
            </tr>

        </table>
    </form>

    </body>
</html>
```

Output

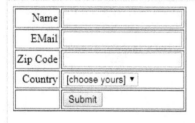

Basic Form Validation

First let us see how to do a basic form validation. In the above form, we are calling **validate()** to validate data when **onsubmit** event is occurring. The following code shows the implementation of this validate() function.

```
<script type="text/javascript">
   <!--
      // Form validation code will come here.
      function validate()
      {

         if( document.myForm.Name.value == "" )
         {
            alert( "Please provide your name!" );
            document.myForm.Name.focus() ;
            return false;
         }

         if( document.myForm.EMail.value == "" )
         {
            alert( "Please provide your Email!" );
            document.myForm.EMail.focus() ;
            return false;
         }

         if( document.myForm.Zip.value == "" ||
         isNaN( document.myForm.Zip.value ) ||
         document.myForm.Zip.value.length != 5 )
         {
            alert( "Please provide a zip in the format #####."
);
            document.myForm.Zip.focus() ;
            return false;
         }
```

```
        if( document.myForm.Country.value == "-1" )
        {
            alert( "Please provide your country!" );
            return false;
        }
        return( true );
    }
  //-->
</script>
```

Data Format Validation

Now we will see how we can validate our entered form data before submitting it to the web server.

The following example shows how to validate an entered email address. An email address must contain at least a '@' sign and a dot (.). Also, the '@' must not be the first character of the email address, and the last dot must at least be one character after the '@' sign.

Example

Try the following code for email validation.

```
<script type="text/javascript">
  <!--
    function validateEmail()
    {
        var emailID = document.myForm.EMail.value;
        atpos = emailID.indexOf("@");
        dotpos = emailID.lastIndexOf(".");

        if (atpos < 1 || ( dotpos - atpos < 2 ))
        {
```

```
        alert("Please enter correct email ID")
        document.myForm.EMail.focus() ;
        return false;
     }
     return( true );
  }
  //-->
</script>
```

JavaScript - Animation

You can use JavaScript to create a complex animation having, but not limited to, the following elements –

- Fireworks
- Fade Effect
- Roll-in or Roll-out
- Page-in or Page-out
- Object movements

You might be interested in existing JavaScript based animation library: Script.Aculo.us.

This tutorial provides a basic understanding of how to use JavaScript to create an animation.

JavaScript can be used to move a number of DOM elements (<img />, <div> or any other HTML element) around the page according to some sort of pattern determined by a logical equation or function.

JavaScript provides the following two functions to be frequently used in animation programs.

- **setTimeout(function, duration)** – This function calls **function**after **duration** milliseconds from now.
- **setInterval(function, duration)** – This function calls **function** after every **duration** milliseconds.
- **clearTimeout(setTimeout_variable)** – This function calls clears any timer set by the setTimeout() functions.

JavaScript can also set a number of attributes of a DOM object including its position on the screen. You can set *top* and left attribute of an object to position it anywhere on the screen. Here is its syntax.

```
// Set distance from left edge of the screen.
object.style.left = distance in pixels or points;
```

or

```
// Set distance from top edge of the screen.
object.style.top = distance in pixels or points;
```

Manual Animation

So let's implement one simple animation using DOM object properties and JavaScript functions as follows. The following list contains different DOM methods.

- We are using the JavaScript function **getElementById()** to get a DOM object and then assigning it to a global variable **imgObj**.
- We have defined an initialization function **init()** to initialize **imgObj** where we have set its **position** and **left** attributes.
- We are calling initialization function at the time of window load.
- Finally, we are calling **moveRight()** function to increase the left distance by 10 pixels. You could also set it to a negative value to move it to the left side.

Example

Try the following example.

```html
<html>
    <head>
        <title>JavaScript Animation</title>
        <script type="text/javascript">
            <!--
                var imgObj = null;
                            function init(){
                    imgObj = document.getElementById('myImage');
                    imgObj.style.position= 'relative';
                    imgObj.style.left = '0px';
                }
                            function moveRight(){
                    imgObj.style.left = parseInt(imgObj.style.left)
+ 10 + 'px';
                }

                window.onload =init;
            //-->
        </script>

    </head>

    <body>

        <form>
            <img id="myImage" src="/images/html.gif" />
            <p>Click button below to move the image to right</p>
            <input type="button" value="Click Me"
onclick="moveRight();" />
        </form>

    </body>
</html>
```

Output

Click button below to move the image to right

[Click Me]

Automated Animation

In the above example, we saw how an image moves to right with every click. We can automate this process by using the JavaScript function **setTimeout( )**as follows −

Here we have added more methods. So let's see what is new here −

- The **moveRight( )** function is calling **setTimeout( )** function to set the position of *imgObj*.
- We have added a new function **stop( )** to clear the timer set by **setTimeout( )** function and to set the object at its initial position.

Example

Try the following example code.

```html
<html>

    <head>
        <title>JavaScript Animation</title>

        <script type="text/javascript">
            <!--
                var imgObj = null;
                var animate ;

                function init(){
                    imgObj = document.getElementById('myImage');
                    imgObj.style.position= 'relative';
                    imgObj.style.left = '0px';
                }

                function moveRight(){
```

```
                imgObj.style.left = parseInt(imgObj.style.left)
+ 10 + 'px';
                animate = setTimeout(moveRight,20); // call
moveRight in 20msec
                }

            function stop(){
                clearTimeout(animate);
                imgObj.style.left = '0px';
            }

            window.onload =init;
        //-->
        </script>

    </head>

    <body>

        <form>
            <img id="myImage" src="/images/html.gif" />
            <p>Click the buttons below to handle animation</p>
            <input type="button" value="Start"
onclick="moveRight();" />
            <input type="button" value="Stop" onclick="stop();" />
        </form>

    </body>
</html>
```

Rollover with a Mouse Event

Here is a simple example showing image rollover with a mouse event.

Let's see what we are using in the following example −

- At the time of loading this page, the 'if' statement checks for the existence of the image object. If the image object is unavailable, this block will not be executed.
- The **Image()** constructor creates and preloads a new image object called **image1**.
- The src property is assigned the name of the external image file called /images/html.gif.
- Similarly, we have created **image2** object and assigned /images/http.gif in this object.
- The # (hash mark) disables the link so that the browser does not try to go to a URL when clicked. This link is an image.
- The **onMouseOver** event handler is triggered when the user's mouse moves onto the link, and the **onMouseOut** event handler is triggered when the user's mouse moves away from the link (image).
- When the mouse moves over the image, the HTTP image changes from the first image to the second one. When the mouse is moved away from the image, the original image is displayed.

- When the mouse is moved away from the link, the initial image html.gif will reappear on the screen.

```html
<html>

    <head>
        <title>Rollover with a Mouse Events</title>

        <script type="text/javascript">
            <!--
                if(document.images){
                    var image1 = new Image(); // Preload an image
                    image1.src = "/images/html.gif";
                    var image2 = new Image(); // Preload second image
                    image2.src = "/images/http.gif";
                }
            //-->
        </script>

    </head>

    <body>
        <p>Move your mouse over the image to see the result</p>

        <a href="#"
onMouseOver="document.myImage.src=image2.src;"
onMouseOut="document.myImage.src=image1.src;">
            <img name="myImage" src="/images/html.gif" />
        </a>
    </body>
</html>
```

JavaScript - Multimedia

The JavaScript **navigator** object includes a child object called **plugins**. This object is an array, with one entry for each plug-in installed on the browser. The navigator.plugins object is supported only by Netscape, Firefox, and Mozilla only.

Example

Here is an example that shows how to list down all the plug-on installed in your browser −

```
<html>

    <head>
        <title>List of Plug-Ins</title>
    </head>

    <body>
        <table border="1">
            <tr>
                <th>Plug-in Name</th>
                <th>Filename</th>
                <th>Description</th>
            </tr>

            <script language="JavaScript" type="text/javascript">
                for (i=0; i<navigator.plugins.length; i++) {
                    document.write("<tr><td>");
                    document.write(navigator.plugins[i].name);
                    document.write("</td><td>");
                    document.write(navigator.plugins[i].filename);
                    document.write("</td><td>");

document.write(navigator.plugins[i].description);
```

```
            document.write("</td></tr>");
        }
    </script>

    </table>

    </body>
</html>
```

Output

Plug-in Name	Filename	Description
Widevine Content Decryption Module	widevinecdmadapter.dll	Enables Widevine licenses for playback of HTML audio/video content. (version: 1.4.8.1000)
Chrome PDF Viewer	mhjfbmdgcfjbbpaeojofohoefgiehjai	
Native Client	internal-nacl-plugin	
Chrome PDF Viewer	internal-pdf-viewer	Portable Document Format

Checking for Plug-Ins

Each plug-in has an entry in the array. Each entry has the following properties

- **name** – is the name of the plug-in.
- **filename** – is the executable file that was loaded to install the plug-in.
- **description** – is a description of the plug-in, supplied by the developer.
- **mimeTypes** – is an array with one entry for each MIME type supported by the plug-in.

You can use these properties in a script to find out the installed plug-ins, and then using JavaScript, you can play appropriate multimedia file. Take a look at the following example.

```
<html>

    <head>
        <title>Using Plug-Ins</title>
    </head>

    <body>

        <script language="JavaScript" type="text/javascript">
            media = navigator.mimeTypes["video/quicktime"];

            if (media){
                document.write("<embed src='quick.mov' height=100
width=100>");
            }
            else
```

```
         {
            document.write("<img src='quick.gif' height=100
width=100>");
         }
      </script>

   </body>
</html>
```

Output

NOTE – Here we are using HTML <embed> tag to embed a multimedia

file.

Controlling Multimedia

Let us take one real example which works in almost all the browsers −

```html
<html>

   <head>
      <title>Using Embeded Object</title>

      <script type="text/javascript">
         <!--
            function play()
            {
               if (!document.demo.IsPlaying()){
               document.demo.Play();
               }
            }
            function stop()
            {
               if (document.demo.IsPlaying()){
               document.demo.StopPlay();
               }
            }
            function rewind()
            {
               if (document.demo.IsPlaying()){
               document.demo.StopPlay();
               }
               document.demo.Rewind();
            }
         //-->
      </script>

   </head>

   <body>
```

```
<embed id="demo" name="demo"
src="http://www.amrood.com/games/kumite.swf"
width="318" height="300" play="false" loop="false"
pluginspage="http://www.macromedia.com/go/getflashplayer"
swliveconnect="true">
</embed>

<form name="form" id="form" action="#" method="get">
    <input type="button" value="Start" onclick="play();"
/>
    <input type="button" value="Stop" onclick="stop();" />
    <input type="button" value="Rewind"
onclick="rewind();" />
</form>

</body>
</html>
```

Output

If you are using Mozilla, Firefox or Netscape, then

JavaScript - Debugging

Every now and then, developers commit mistakes while coding. A mistake in a program or a script is referred to as a **bug**.

The process of finding and fixing bugs is called **debugging** and is a normal part of the development process. This section covers tools and techniques that can help you with debugging tasks..

Error Messages in IE

The most basic way to track down errors is by turning on error information in your browser. By default, Internet Explorer shows an error icon in the status bar when an error occurs on the page.

Double-clicking this icon takes you to a dialog box showing information about the specific error that occurred.

Since this icon is easy to overlook, Internet Explorer gives you the option to automatically show the Error dialog box whenever an error occurs.

To enable this option, select Tools → Internet Options → Advanced tab.and then finally check the **"Display a Notification About Every Script Error"** box option as shown below –

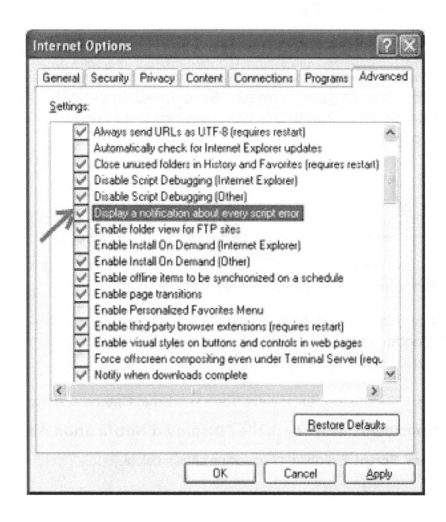

Error Messages in Firefox or Mozilla

Other browsers like Firefox, Netscape, and Mozilla send error messages to a special window called the **JavaScript Console** or **Error Consol**. To view the console, select **Tools → Error Consol** or **Web Development**.

Unfortunately, since these browsers give no visual indication when an error occurs, you must keep the Console open and watch for errors as your script executes.

Error Notifications

Error notifications that show up on Console or through Internet Explorer dialog boxes are the result of both syntax and runtime errors. These error notification include the line number at which the error occurred.

If you are using Firefox, then you can click on the error available in the error console to go to the exact line in the script having error.

How to debug a Script

There are various ways to debug your JavaScript –

Use a JavaScript Validator

One way to check your JavaScript code for strange bugs is to run it through a program that checks it to make sure it is valid and that it follows the official syntax rules of the language. These programs are called **validating parsers**or just **validators** for short, and often come with commercial HTML and JavaScript editors.

The most convenient validator for JavaScript is Douglas Crockford's JavaScript Lint, which is available for free at Douglas Crockford's JavaScript Lint.

Simply visit that web page, paste your JavaScript (Only JavaScript) code into the text area provided, and click the jslint button. This program will parse through your JavaScript code, ensuring that all the variable and function definitions follow the correct syntax. It will also check JavaScript statements, such as if and **while,** to ensure they too follow the correct format

Add Debugging Code to Your Programs

You can use the **alert()** or **document.write()** methods in your program to debug your code. For example, you might write something as follows −

```
var debugging = true;
var whichImage = "widget";

if( debugging )
alert( "Calls swapImage() with argument: " + whichImage );
var swapStatus = swapImage( whichImage );

if( debugging )
    alert( "Exits swapImage() with swapStatus=" + swapStatus );
```

By examining the content and order of the **alert()** as they appear, you can examine the health of your program very easily.

Use a JavaScript Debugger

A debugger is an application that places all aspects of script execution under the control of the programmer. Debuggers provide fine-grained control over the state of the script through an interface that allows you to examine and set values as well as control the flow of execution.

Once a script has been loaded into a debugger, it can be run one line at a time or instructed to halt at certain breakpoints. Once execution is halted, the programmer can examine the state of the script and its variables in order to determine if something is amiss. You can also watch variables for changes in their values.

The latest version of the Mozilla JavaScript Debugger (code-named Venkman) for both Mozilla and Netscape browsers can be downloaded at http://www.hacksrus.com/~ginda/venkman

Useful tips for developers

You can keep the following tips in mind to reduce the number of errors in your scripts and simplify the debugging process –

- Use plenty of **comments**. Comments enable you to explain why you wrote the script the way you did and to explain particularly difficult sections of code.
- Always use **indentation** to make your code easy to read. Indenting statements also makes it easier for you to match up beginning and ending tags, curly braces, and other HTML and script elements.
- Write **modular code**. Whenever possible, group your statements into functions. Functions let you group related statements, and test and reuse portions of code with minimal effort.
- Be consistent in the way you name your variables and functions. Try using names that are long enough to be meaningful and that describe the contents of the variable or the purpose of the function.
- Use consistent syntax when naming variables and functions. In other words, keep them all lowercase or all uppercase; if you prefer Camel-Back notation, use it consistently.
- **Test long scripts** in a modular fashion. In other words, do not try to write the entire script before testing any portion of it. Write a piece and get it to work before adding the next portion of code.
- Use **descriptive variable and function names** and avoid using single-character names.
- **Watch your quotation marks**. Remember that quotation marks are used in pairs around strings and that both

245

quotation marks must be of the same style (either single or double).

- **Watch your equal signs**. You should not used a single = for comparison purpose.
- Declare **variables explicitly** using the **var** keyword.

JavaScript - Image Map

You can use JavaScript to create client-side image map. Client-side image maps are enabled by the **usemap** attribute for the <img /> tag and defined by special <map> and <area> extension tags.

The image that is going to form the map is inserted into the page using the <img /> element as normal, except that it carries an extra attribute called **usemap**. The value of the usemap attribute is the value of the name attribute on the <map> element, which you are about to meet, preceded by a pound or hash sign.

The <map> element actually creates the map for the image and usually follows directly after the <img /> element. It acts as a container for the <area /> elements that actually define the clickable hotspots. The <map> element carries only one attribute, the **name** attribute, which is the name that identifies the map. This is how the <img /> element knows which <map> element to use.

The <area> element specifies the shape and the coordinates that define the boundaries of each clickable hotspot.

The following code combines imagemaps and JavaScript to produce a message in a text box when the mouse is moved over different parts of an image.

```html
<html>

   <head>
      <title>Using JavaScript Image Map</title>

      <script type="text/javascript">
         <!--
            function showTutorial(name){
               document.myform.stage.value = name
            }
         //-->
      </script>

   </head>

   <body>
      <form name="myform">
         <input type="text" name="stage" size="20" />
      </form>

      <!-- Create  Mappings -->
      <img src="/images/usemap.gif" alt="HTML Map" border="0"
usemap="#tutorials"/>

      <map name="tutorials">
         <area shape="poly"
            coords="74,0,113,29,98,72,52,72,38,27"
            href="/perl/index.htm" alt="Perl Tutorial"
            target="_self"
            onMouseOver="showTutorial('perl')"
            onMouseOut="showTutorial('')"/>

         <area shape="rect"
```

```
            coords="22,83,126,125"
            href="/html/index.htm" alt="HTML Tutorial"
            target="_self"
            onMouseOver="showTutorial('html')"
            onMouseOut="showTutorial('')"/>

        <area shape="circle"
            coords="73,168,32"
            href="/php/index.htm" alt="PHP Tutorial"
            target="_self"
            onMouseOver="showTutorial('php')"
            onMouseOut="showTutorial('')"/>
    </map>
  </body>
</html>
```

Output

You can feel the map concept by placing the mouse cursor on
the image object.

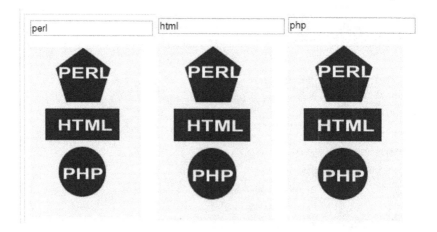

JavaScript - Browsers Compatibility

It is important to understand the differences between different browsers in order to handle each in the way it is expected. So it is important to know which browser your web page is running in.

To get information about the browser your webpage is currently running in, use the built-in **navigator** object.

Navigator Properties

There are several Navigator related properties that you can use in your Web page. The following is a list of the names and descriptions of each.

Sr.No	Property & Des0063ription
1	**appCodeName** This property is a string that contains the code name of the browser, Netscape for Netscape and Microsoft Internet Explorer for Internet Explorer.

2	**appVersion** This property is a string that contains the version of the browser as well as other useful information such as its language and compatibility.
3	**language** This property contains the two-letter abbreviation for the language that is used by the browser. Netscape only.
4	**mimTypes[]** This property is an array that contains all MIME types supported by the client. Netscape only.
5	**platform[]** This property is a string that contains the platform for which the browser was compiled."Win32" for 32-bit Windows operating systems
6	**plugins[]** This property is an array containing all the plug-ins that have been installed on the client. Netscape only.
7	**userAgent[]** This property is a string that contains the code name and version of the browser. This value is sent to the originating server to identify the client.

Navigator Methods

There are several Navigator-specific methods. Here is a list of their names and descriptions.

Sr.No	Description
1	**javaEnabled()** This method determines if JavaScript is enabled in the client. If JavaScript is enabled, this method returns true; otherwise, it returns false.
2	**plugings.refresh** This method makes newly installed plug-ins available and populates the plugins array with all new plug-in names. Netscape only.
3	**preference(name,value)** This method allows a signed script to get and set some Netscape preferences. If the second parameter is omitted, this method will return the value of the specified preference; otherwise, it sets the value. Netscape only.
4	**taintEnabled()** This method returns true if data tainting is enabled; false otherwise.

Browser Detection

There is a simple JavaScript which can be used to find out the name of a browser and then accordingly an HTML page can be served to the user.

```
<html>

   <head>
      <title>Browser Detection Example</title>
   </head>

   <body>

      <script type="text/javascript">
         <!--
            var userAgent   = navigator.userAgent;
            var opera       = (userAgent.indexOf('Opera') != -
1);
            var ie          = (userAgent.indexOf('MSIE') != -
1);
            var gecko       = (userAgent.indexOf('Gecko') != -
1);
            var netscape    = (userAgent.indexOf('Mozilla') !=
-1);
            var version     = navigator.appVersion;

            if (opera){
               document.write("Opera based browser");
               // Keep your opera specific URL here.
            }

            else if (gecko){
               document.write("Mozilla based browser");
               // Keep your gecko specific URL here.
            }
```

```
        else if (ie){
            document.write("IE based browser");
            // Keep your IE specific URL here.
        }

        else if (netscape){
            document.write("Netscape based browser");
            // Keep your Netscape specific URL here.
        }

        else{
            document.write("Unknown browser");
        }
        // You can include version to along with any above
condition.
        document.write("<br /> Browser version info : " +
version );
        //-->
    </script>

    </body>
</html>
```

Output

Mozilla based browser
Browser version info : 5.0 (Windows NT 6.1; Win64; x64)
AppleWebKit/537.36 (KHTML, like Gecko) Chrome/60.0.3112.113
Safari/537.36